M

Waking Up In
CHIC

JL

Printed in the United Kingdom by MPG Books Ltd, Bodmin, Cornwall

Published by Sanctuary Publishing Limited, Sanctuary House, 45–53 Sinclair Road,
London W14 0NS, United Kingdom

www.sanctuarypublishing.com

ISBN: 1-86074-558-X

Waking Up In
CHICAGO

Claire Hughes

Sanctuary

Contents

Acknowledgements

Thanks to all the Chicago people I spoke to for this book, especially Mike at Premonition Records, Bob Koester, Bruce Iglauer, Ben at The Jazz Institute, Derrick Carter and Duke.

For everything, always, thanks to my husband Jonny...

Claire Hughes, December 2003

1 Duke's Bench

EVERY DAY Duke sits on the same dark green wooden bench, just one of the six that face inwards towards the small stone fountain at the intersection of Division, Milwaukee and Ashland in the city of Chicago. 24-hour traffic revs at high speeds along these three long, frantic streets and screeches to a halt in tune with the stop light system. Drivers beep their horns. Cyclists weave in and out of the bedlam. Pedestrians battle their way across the road and cop car sirens wail but here, in the centre of it all, there's a comforting lull, eased by the sound of water trickling from the fountain. In the height of summer, after 3pm once the cooler hours have set in, a hunched-over vendor wheels a cart into the square piled high with hunks of sticky honeycomb, sugared nuts and candy-coloured sweets. The vendor brings his own fold-away stool and for the rest of the day and well into the evening he sits by the trolley. There he stays, waiting for people going out of and into the subway opening that sits on the Ashland side of the triangle, or general passers by who might want to buy. Opposite that, running along the Milwaukee side of the space, is a cab stop where drivers wait for pick-ups.

In the middle of the relentless, noisy traffic, in this unlikely urban oasis in the near West Side of the city, a little community of people works out its daily routine. Of all these people, Duke is my favourite. His expression rarely seems to change. Sparkly dark eyes are shrouded by thick folds of dark flesh that spread out into his nose and gather into an amiable, mock-stern pucker around his mouth. He's always dressed smartly, sometimes in a battered cotton suit and others in loose trousers and shirt. On his head, over a soft down of white hair, is a cool cotton peak cap and on his feet he wears cosy-looking, soft-leather, open-toed sandals. Duke's only accessory is a thick, wooden stick with a rubber stop at the end. In all the times I've walked past him on the way to the subway, or dashed by his bench to grab a taxi, I've never seen him do anything else but sit there, still as the stone fountain he faces. Sometimes, when the heat is choking, children play in the fountain and their splashes send drops of water alarmingly close to Duke's ankles – but he doesn't flinch. In fall, when the air cools, the maple leaves are orange-red and the children are gone, Duke is still there on his bench. In fact it's only when the fountain is frozen over and the icy winter winds have chased even the vendor away that Duke's bench lies empty.

It's during those short, cold, unforgiving days that the city lives up to its 'Windy' moniker and the gusts that blast across Chicago from Lake Michigan and right up Division cut through you like icy blades. Set in the middle of North America, the 227 sc .are miles that make up Chicago serve as the focal point for the sprawling Mid West of the United States. It might be just the third biggest city in America but as the biggest urban spot in 'the prairie', as natives like to call it, Chicago has always been the place where people end up when they leave their country towns for the fast life. Anyone from the Mid West searching for the 'bright lights big city' urban setting will probably make it to Chicago before they get to New York or Los Angeles. Chicago seems more manageable somehow. Set well apart from the affluent West Coast and the cutting edge East Coast of America, the city has its own identity, flavoured by the diverse cultures and creeds of around 10 million people packed tightly into the city's back-on-back neighbourhoods.

I wandered through a lot of Chicago districts, eating, drinking, listening to music, shopping, sitting, staring and idling – but it didn't take me long to work out that Wicker Park was the one for me. On the near West Side of the city and right next to Bucktown, its understated chic, cosy restaurants and bustling nightlife were like a welcoming hug to an out-of-towner like me. It's never been the glitz of a city that I've been after – that's just something to dip in and out of when you feel like it. All the reasons I love city life can be found in a city neighbourhood like Wicker Park. Here in the hubbub of a hotchpotch grid of streets and cramped-up houses are wedged a range of creeds and cultures that make the area impossible to define in terms of one belief or persuasion. In a city neighbourhood you can be anyone and no-one at the same time. And yet, if you hang out for long enough, you'll get to know people around you and before long you'll become, quite simply, yourself.

THE REASON I knew Duke was called Duke was because we actually spoke one day. I had come out of the subway and was so knocked back by the searing heat that I took a moment to sit down next to him on his bench. The fountain was bubbling and the shade from the maple trees dappling the bench and warm tarmac in front of it. Sitting down on his bench, I could feel what made Duke's spot so desirable. Here in the cool shade of the trees the traffic, though only yards away, seemed light years from us and the sound of the water in the fountain was instantly soothing. I turned to Duke and asked him the time. He turned his head slowly and looked at me, his old eyes sparkling out of his ancient, well-lined face. For a moment he looked as if he wasn't going to answer. Then he looked slowly down at his leather-strapped wrist watch, looked back up at me and said, in a voice that sounded as soothing as the trickling water from the fountain and as old as the city itself: 'a quarter after three'. I knew that anyway. I was just trying to make conversation.

'I see you sitting here every day,' I said.
'Yes you do,' he said.
'I can understand why.'
'Me too.'
'What's your name?'
'Duke.'

And that was it. For the next hour or so we shot the breeze there on Duke's bench. He told me that this area, Wicker Park – so-called because there is a big park called Wicker Park slap bang in the middle of it – used to be a rough neighbourhood until a few years ago. He told me he'd lived here pretty much all his life, worked hard all his life and now was his time to 'kick back'.

'Life is hard in this city,' he said. 'But Chicago people, we keep each other going.'

Go east along Division, just south of Duke's bench, and the second street on the left is Greenview – and that's where I woke up every morning. My apartment was in the top floor of a pretty townhouse owned by a Mexican-American artist and his Polish-American film-maker wife. My comfy little bedroom was at the front of the house; it opened out onto a living room area that tapered into a narrow hallway off which came the bathroom/washroom and a kitchenette at the end. Out back was a wooden porch (a staple for most Chicago homes) and here in the evenings I would sit and look out over the city just as hundreds of other Chicagoans did on each night of the city's long hot summers. My apartment looked out over a sunken garden where an apricot tree heavy with creamy-peachy fruit and a wizened old grapevine clung together in the sultry shade like secret lovers. Even in the midday heat that garden stayed cool and whenever I sat underneath the apricot tree hiding from the scorching sun, the strains and stresses of city life would disperse, carried away on the soft whispers of the ancient vine.

Chicago winters are cruel with temperatures often plummeting to 20 degrees below zero. Icy winds rage across the prairie or off Lake Michigan and tear through the city's neighbourhoods, making it feel 20, sometimes 30 degrees below that. But from June until October every year, the weather is as beautiful as it can be and as far as summer in the city goes, there aren't many places better. I'd visited Chicago in winter. I'd done a short stint in autumn too but it was during that first summer that I finally got acquainted with the city.

JUST 10 years ago life in Wicker Park was different. Like many cities Chicago is ever evolving, with areas once rough and dangerous regenerating and bringing in an influx of high earners who buy up the property, open up bars and restaurants and clean up the district. That regeneration happened to Wicker Park back in the early Nineties. By the time I arrived there, a decade later, the edge was coming off the place and it felt as if the streets and blocks that made up the neighbourhood were relaxing into each other and moving at a natural tempo.

Northeast of Duke's bench on Milwaukee is where the hubbub of Wicker Park kicks in and collides with the beginnings of Ukrainian Village. The Empty Bottle on 1035 N Western Street, when it opened here in those early regeneration days, injected a musical burst into the neighbourhood and now, every night of the week, it's where local jazz ensembles and home-town alt-rock bands play. Another rock spot is the Double Door at 1572 Milwaukee where The Rolling Stones famously performed. Nearby is dance club Red Dog where house music is spun by local DJs every night of the week. West of Duke's bench on Division is Smoke Daddy where you can get racks of barbecue ribs, hot, crispy fries and cold beer all day and night. Every evening at Smoke Daddy, you can hear live blues music with local bands, singers and even poets squeezed onto the elevated stage in the corner of the restaurant by the door. Further northwest from Smoke Daddy is the beginning of the Bucktown area, another recent regeneration hot spot with restaurants, shops, bars and clubs.

The area is rife with record stores. House music emporium Gramaphone Records is in Bucktown, at 2663 N Clark Street, a shop where many of the city's best-known house music DJs and producers worked for a stint. Weekend Records & Soap at 1919 West Division is a record and soap shop, run by neo-electro producer Magus and his soap-maker wife. Minutes from Duke's bench, at 1120 N Ashland Street, is Dusty Groove Records, specialising in hip hop and Brazilian music. Reckless Records is nearby at 2055 W North Avenue and here you can get new and used music across-the-board. Right next to Reckless is a small café/bookstore called Myopic Books that is the focal point for a weekly, improvised music series that had been running in the city since the mid-Nineties. It's out of this 'Myopic scene' that alternative Chicago bands like Town & Country, US Maple and Pillow got to meet. A local label called Box Media released a series of 'Myopic

Sessions' albums during the mid-late Nineties. Town & Country was originally signed to Box Media and then got picked up by local label Thrill Jockey, also home to alternative Chicago rock bands Sea & Cake and Tortoise. Many of the players who have been involved with Tortoise over the years played down at the Myopic. The Monday night improvised sessions down at the bookstore used to be run by a local drummer called Michael Zurang. He stopped doing those at the end of the Nineties, though, and now he runs jazz/improvised music nights at a place called the Candlestick Maker, in the northwest of the city at 4432 North Kedzie. The space is an old rubber stamp store where Michael now lives: if you want to be fussy about it, it probably falls into a 'grey' area when it comes to legality. The place makes it into the listings guide of local free rag the *Reader* but its location on Kedzie isn't clearly posted. If you're looking for it, someone told me, 'just look for the rubber stamp sign'. Michael presents music in his front room, which is also the old shop front. But even without Michael's Monday nights, the Myopic scene is still strong. The bookstore has moved three or four times since it opened and now it's here in the heart of Bucktown, not far from Duke's bench.

It took me a while to discover the benefits of my immediate area after arriving in Chicago but once I did I finally understood why Duke sat on that bench every day. In that tranquil spot, he was slap bang in the middle of three of Chicago's most vibrant neighbourhoods, with all kinds of sights, sounds, flavours and people right at his fingertips. If he ever wanted or needed to reach out and touch them, that is.

From my spot on Greenview, Division Street is a fairly good spot from which to start in terms of working out the layout of the city. Go northwest on Division as far as you can and you'll end up in the suburb of Evanston. Head out the other direction, though, and the road takes you downtown and pretty much directly onto the yellow sandy beach at the shore of Lake Michigan. On the day I'd first spoken to Duke, he'd described the layout of the city.

'You got the North, South and West Side of Chicago but there ain't no East Side 'cos that's just the lake,' he said. 'Go as far east on Division as you can and you'll end up there.'

So I did.

From the end of Division I walked about five blocks, into a concrete underpass which dived below the wide-set, lake-hugging Lake Shore Drive – and suddenly I was in roller-blade heaven. A wide, flat promenade trims this part of the 1,660-mile-long beach that circles Lake Michigan and along this thick, hot strip of white concrete, on that hot, sunny day, Chicago, Illinois suddenly became Chicago, California.

Understanding how Chicago works isn't easy. Like most US cities, of course, its grid system makes the street layout and areas easy to work out in a few days. But, like most cities across the world, the real story is a lot more complex than any map could ever reveal in its lines and stops. In his film *Halsted Street, USA*, David E Simpson chooses to define Chicago by slicing it right down the middle – and the place where he makes his cut is a street called Halsted. This long street, just like many others in Chicago, stretches from the south to the north of the city. But Halsted is different in so many ways. It begins on the banks of the Ohio River in the south of the county, runs up to the city's southern edge and then right through most of Chicago. It's a street, says Simpson in his film, 'torn apart by class and ethnic divisions', and you don't have to spend long in the city to realise that could be a fair description of Chicago itself. Simpson suggests in his film that Chicago is an 'American melting pot at full boil' – and it's here, on Halsted Street, that we get a taste of all the ingredients that make up the heady concoction.

In his film Simpson calls Chicago 'one of the most segregated cities in the US' and picks out 'certain neighbourhoods where white man is not allowed after dark'. Local knowledge is the key here and it's not immediately obvious which neighbourhoods Simpson means. But Halsted, on its journey south to north across Chicago, cuts through some of the most notoriously dangerous districts in the city.

One of these is the Cabrini Green area around 1600 North Halsted. This area, stuck right in the centre of a more affluent part of the city, has, according to locals, always been a trouble spot. Towering buildings shade the streets and on every corner of every block, it seems, there's a liquor store or a burned-out car. Recently city officials have been pouring money into the area, building local sports centres and play areas for kids. But back in the early 1990s, the first strains of Chicago's homegrown hip hop scene emerged in this edgy and violent neighbourhood. The city's first house music revolution in the Eighties – a revolution with black, urban roots in Chicago – had left behind raw, stripped-down, electronically generated blips and bleeps and these took on a new theme in Cabrini Green in the Nineties. If you drove through the area in those days, you could hear the pulse and rhythm of funky, raw-sounding, tough bassline-helmed tracks pounding from small, rectangular windows in the high-rise slabs. It was these cobbled together tracks that marked the first strains of hip house and later helped ignite the city's hip hop scene, converting a whole host of youths from Chicago who were looking for a sound that was more relevant to life in a troubled urban sprawl. Rap music comes from the streets and Chicago rap, like every other strain of music that comes out of the city, is functional, home-made and home-played in a way that you'll find in no other city in America. This musical functionality is unique to Chicago and it's a trait that existed way before hip hop culture came to the city.

The big band era of the early 1900s spawned the first jazz music and it was in Chicago that much of that music was played, listened to and danced to. Ragtime piano music – a syncopated evolution of march music – started appearing before that in the late 1800s and was also a strong feature of Chicago's nightlife in that period. It's as difficult to identify the origins of jazz as it is to define the form – but Chicago is a good place to start if you're looking for the answer to both questions. Since the early 20th century, jazz and blues have been inextricably linked and in the South Side area of Chicago, these serpentine sounds filled the air. Dances like the Chameleon and the Charleston were tailored to this ragtime-jazz period. The Charleston emerged on the stage in theatres in Chicago in the early 1920s. Women who danced the Charleston were called 'flappers' because of the way they would flap their arms and walk like birds while performing it. Songs grew around the dance and it became a staple in clubs and theatres in the city.

It was from Chicago that the very first broadcasts of jazz, or 'jass' as it was called then, were made and played live on radio by in-house big bands. In the days before the term 'jazz' existed, piano players like Ferdinand 'Jelly Roll' Morton would bring the bars on 'The Stroll' – an area down South on 49th Street – alive by segueing ragtime and big band sounds into peppier songs, instantly danceable and designed to fuel the city's burgeoning nightlife. Morton was prominent as a musician well before 1917 when the first jazz recordings were made but he didn't actually get into the studio until the 1920s. New Orleans cornet players King Oliver, aka Joe Oliver the 'King Of New Orleans', and Louis Armstrong were based in Chicago for a while during this time and played around the city long before their music was committed to wax.

By the end of the 1920s, Chicago jazz was flourishing but New York had taken over as the focal point for the form. Meanwhile the influx of African-Americans from South to North during the 'great migration' of the early 20th century saw a style of music called 'blues' imported to Chicago and during the 1930s and 1940s the city became a hotbed for this sound. A Chicago-based producer/A&R man called Lester Melrose, who worked for major labels Columbia and Victor, sourced and released music from the city's newly adopted blues artists including Big Bill Broonzy, Memphis Minnie, Washboard Sam and Tampa Red during this fertile period. This output, coupled with the releases from the jazzier blues divas Bessie Smith and Ma Rainey, helped form the early strains of what would later become the 'Chicago Blues' sound.

But Chicago isn't simply known for jazz and blues. It's also the home of gospel and it was here in the city, during that same era, that many of the original gospel songs still sung today in churches the world over were penned by local songwriter Thomas A. Dorsey. In the 1950s, local label Chess Records released some of the earliest R&B tunes that some say kick-started the whole rock 'n' roll revolution. Tunes by Chuck Berry and Ike Turner and The Rhythm King's 'Rocket 88' are cited by artists like The Rolling Stones as THE first rock 'n' roll tunes and they were pressed up and released by Chicago's very own

Chess Records. The 1970s punk movement came across the water from the UK and ignited in the city too, with bands like Naked Raygun and The Effigies creating their own scene. Industrial music and alt-rock has its own self-servicing music scene in the city. And anyone who's into electronic music will know that Chicago is the home of house music, with the Chicago house sound responsible for kick-starting a dance music revolution with seismic reverberations that are still being felt right across the globe. The alt-country movement currently sweeping the US and making ripples in Europe found its footing here in Chicago too, where the scene – based around live hoe-down style gigs and DJ sessions performed by artists on local label Bloodshot Records – is as vibrant as when it emerged in the early Nineties. That's a lot of musical history for a town that has traditionally been very self-deprecating when it comes to past achievements.

When I arrived in Chicago for the first time I couldn't believe how little the city made of its musical landmarks and historical musical achievements. When it comes to music, the past is just as important as the present. The two go together. But here in Chicago it seemed like history was erasable. Many of the old dancehalls and theatres have vanished and turned into car parks. When I spoke to Duke about this he shrugged and said: 'They just pave shit over in the city.' If a car park is what people need then that's what the city will provide and it seems that only tourists are disturbed by this situation. Chicago is one of the most important cities in the world when it comes to modern music. When you arrive in the city, though, you realise that its people are more concerned with just getting on with things.

This is never more apparent than on Halsted Street. Taken as a cross-section of the city, Halsted gives you the real Chicago, in all its various moods. Good neighbourhoods back onto bad, different cultures and creeds live side-by-side, and all are joined together by this definite, long, straight urban fibre. No surprise then that it's right here, in the neighbourhoods that incorporate this street, that some of the most exciting, contemporary music Chicago has to offer is being made. On street corners, in parking lots, in people's houses and in corner bars, the rhymes and rhythms that make up an important part of Chicago's hip hop scene are worked on and spat out.

WIND BACK 20 years and there wasn't a hip hop scene to speak of in the city. The late Seventies b-boy craze had filtered west from New York and, by the beginning of the Eighties, Chicago was beginning to breed its own breakdance crews. Graffiti art began to appear on trains and buildings around this time too but musically, as far as hip hop went, there was very little creativity to be found in the city. By the mid-1990s, university-based radio stations like the University of Chicago's WHPK and Northwestern's WNUR were hosting hip hop-themed shows – but young, fresh, black, urban music in Chicago was still better represented by what was going on in the underground house and budding hip house scenes. But eventually this changed and young, black, Chicago kids from the ghetto who wanted to hear music more relevant to their lives than the house, gospel, jazz, rock and blues music going on in the city, recognised that hip hop, with its rough beats and real lyrics, was the way forward. A DIY scene began in the city, fuelled by rap music from New York and Los Angeles that Chicago kids could buy in a record store called George's Music Room, on 3195 West Roosevelt. George Daniels, the septuagenarian owner of the Music Room, would host guest appearances from hip hop producers from the East and West Coast of America and before long Chicago began to nurture its own artists.

Today, names like Da Brat and Common have put Chicago on the map in terms of rap music. Snapshots of both of these artists, captured on George's 'Wall of Fame' that shows him pictured with most of the US's hip hop greats, hang in a frame right by the front door of the Music Room. But anyone who's made it big on the hip hop scene in Chicago, it seems, has left town to pursue fame and fortune in bigger cities. Today rap music in Chicago enjoys a vibrant scene only on a grass-roots level. There are a few local crews who have become known in the city, like The Molemen, The Nacrobats and The Family Tree. The Molemen has its own label, Molemen Recordings, that has received some attention in the United States. Chicago's All Natural crew, with its combination of precise turntablism and witty rhymes, gained a local following in the late 1990s and got signed to Thrill Jockey, but this is a wild card act on that label.

Without a wide-based, thriving Chicago label devoted entirely to rap, artists coming out of the hip hop scene in the city have little chance of getting a national footing. You can hear rap music on the radio but not much of it is locally made. Whispers of hatred in Chicago's hip hop community reverberate through the neighbourhoods, yet much of the rap music coming out of the city focuses on positives instead of negatives. Chicago's biggest rap export Common (formerly Common Sense) is known for his conscious lyrics, a healthy alternative to the gangsta rap rife in other US cities. The All Natural crew deals in clever rhymes that opt for a sharp yet humorous view on life in the city. This positive take on life through music is a Chicago thing – and yet little of this Chicago hip hop sound penetrates outside the city. Clubs across the city host open mic sessions, there's hip hop jams most nights of the week, DJs play in clubs over the North, West and South sides – and yet the city isn't known for its rap music per se. Things are a lot better than they were ten years ago but there's still a long way to go.

In cities like New York, Los Angeles, Atlanta, Oakland, New Orleans and Detroit, rap music has also developed its own identity. In each one of these cities, however, rap enjoys a strong base via a self-servicing record label that nurtures artists in the city. The problem with Chicago, confirms Project X Records owner Jesse Wordlaw, is that everyone in the city's hip hop scene is battling against each other.

'I think that as far as independent hip hop labels go, everybody wants to be the first label to make it big,' he says. 'We have a lot of artists come from Chicago like Da Brat, Common, Crucial Conflict, Do Or Die – a lot of artists from Chicago but there's no label. New Orleans you think of Cash Money or No Limit, California is Death Row and New York is Bad Bwoy – so there's no independent label here in Chicago to establish Chicago as the home – but that's what we're trying to do here. Really what I'm trying to do is get everyone from Chicago to work together and come together. Let's do it and let's all have one vision and one focus.'

It's what Jesse is trying to do with Project X. He used to be into house music, he says, until he 'grew up', and it's when he first heard music from artists like NWA and Ice T and records like 'Rapper's Delight' that he got switched on to rap. After starting Project X in the early 1990s, Jesse has been slowly grouping together a pool of artists.

'It's just one of those things,' Jesse shrugs. 'My label, I'm thinking in my mind we're going to be the first label to do it. Then there's Raw Dope – they might be thinking they're going to do it. Or Neighborhood Watch thinking they're going to do it – so everybody is kind of almost at the finish line and it's like the race where you get there and you're kind of elbowing each other. The way we do things here, I don't want to do that. I just say to my artists, "if you want to do a song with one of those that's fine". I want to break that barrier down as far as my company is concerned.'

This 'family' of producers, rappers and DJs that come together under Project X are from all over the city. The thread is Jesse and through him they have found a way to get their music and lyrics out there. Jesse is from the South Side of Chicago and it's in those parts that he found girl rapper A'Sista who recently released her debut album 'What If' through Project X. A'Sista's lyrics are pithy yet insightful. Her subject matter is drawn from the struggles of a young woman's life in the city but her spin on the subject suggests a lot more experience than her 24 years would suggest. When I meet up with her at a café on East Lake Street, beneath the rumbling bellow of the El train's elevated tracks, I don't expect to find the petite, pretty, smiley-faced young woman who is sitting in front of a glass of water at the window table. The quick-fire lyrics on her record surely can't come from the same lips that smile while mouthing the words 'are you Claire?' across the café to me. She waves me into the seat opposite her, I sit down and the first thing I want to know is how she got into rapping in the first place.

'I started when I was about 13. I used to rap in a girl group called Katastrophe with a friend of mine. We rapped for a while, throughout high school, and then went our separate ways and I eventually went ahead and went solo. Back then we would do open mics, a lot of talent shows and stuff. I used to rap about a lot of things I was going through. Female issues as far as how we felt we stood in the rap game as women. We had a lot of fun songs too. We had one song called "Don't Let It Get You Down Girl" about women coming up and having a hard time in life but getting through it anyway, heads up. So it was kind of pretty much the same stuff that I'm rapping about now but it was just a little different because I was a little girl then and I wasn't really experiencing stuff. I was just envisioning other people experiencing those things.'

A'Sista has lived on the South Side of Chicago pretty much all her life. It was around 49th Street on the South Side that jazz music had its heyday in the 1920s. Since then, though, that street, and the streets that slip down from there into the 'wild hundreds' as she calls them, have turned into downtrodden residential areas. Ask anyone who lives in the north of the city and they'll say that the South Side is a no-go area after dark. Heading down towards the 'wild hundreds' is something you get warned against doing by Chicago folk.

'It's just a little wild down there I guess,' she smiles. 'For instance, if you go up north it's more cool and calm. They have stuff like the Navy Pier but back down in the wild hundreds it's a little rougher. The neighbourhoods are rougher. There's a bit of gunslinging but there's more poverty. More drugs and gangs and stuff like that. It does depress me a little bit sometimes but my music helps me look past that. I ride the bus back and forth from home a lot and if I see some stuff going on that's negative, that helps me in a way and I start writing. It's just a way to get a lot of stuff off my chest. I know I don't want to be in that type of environment for a long time, so this is something I want to move further with.'

Hip hop has traditionally been male-dominated. In rap lyrics a woman is, quite often, either a 'bitch' or a 'ho' and there are very few female rappers out there who use their voices to dispel this negative image. As far as A'Sista is concerned, that's a big problem that extends from the music into life in general.

'I think as a woman you experience every type of prejudice: racism, sexism and all of that,' she says. 'It's tough but I just try to stay focused. That's how I came up with A'Sista 'cos it represents me and women in general. Not necessarily black or white, but it's just women in general. Whatever you think of A'Sista – that's what I am. I didn't want to limit myself because I was representing women as a whole. I had a lot of inspirations too. Tupac Shakur is actually my favourite rapper but as far as female rappers go I used to love MC Lion, Queen Latifah. When they came out I was like "yes, this is finally a chance for women to open the door for us", so I was excited about that. I love Da Brat too. The way that she came out and she was from Chicago too – it just made me really feel "okay I can do this". This is something for me. My other inspirations are people like Marvin Gaye, Stevie Wonder and I like a lot of old school music because a lot of it just really touched me emotionally. A lot of music that I listen to now, it's not as emotional as it was. That's why I go back and I put a Stevie Wonder song on or a Marvin Gaye song or an Isley Brothers song and I'm like "yeah". Even though I was younger back then I just remember those songs from my mom and my older uncles and aunts.

'People say that a lot of the rappers are negative but it just depends what kind of environment they come up from. People respond to the type of energy they get. So if you're a child growing up around a neighbourhood where all you see is negative stuff most likely that's the stuff you're going to talk about. Some people know how to look ahead and cover all angles but when you grow up in that type of environment it's hard to break away from that. I believe that real rap is just about people trying to call out. It's kind of like a way for breaking away from negative energy. Instead of involving themselves in it they decide well, let me talk about it and let people know what's going on around and see if someone else is feeling the same way that I'm feeling.'

A'Sista met Jesse when she was part of Katastrophe. Now, as a solo artist through Project X, she's getting a chance to spread her word and is already known across the city. At open mic sessions, other city kids recognise her. It's not about fame, A'Sista tells me. For her the only message is in her music.

'I just want to put out as much real and positive music as I can,' she says. 'Because I believe that especially with a lot of the female artists out now, they're kind of pushed to come out and be sexy and be a certain way which is designed to appeal to men. It's okay to look good but I really feel like there's more to music than that so I'm trying to bring out a different side of things.'

A'Sista pauses and looks past me towards a twenty-something man with a wide scar running from mouth to ear on the right side of his face who is knocking on the window. He rushes into the café and greets A'Sista.

'Hey, you must be Claire,' he says, his grin cut wider by the rudely healed gash.

I shrug. 'Yes.'

'I'm Heathon,' he says.

Heathon is another of the Project X 'family'. When A'Sista has finished her water, she explains she has to be somewhere else. When she has politely said her goodbyes and made her way out into the hot streets, it's Heathon's turn to tell me his story. As the El growls overhead, casting a deep shadow over the sun-drenched tables in the café, I listen to him spill out his tale at the same frenetic pace as he spits rhymes.

'In all my raps I write about experience. I get real serious in my rap. My brother got killed. My sister is in a penitentiary upstate. She murdered her best friend. She did this on my face too,' he says, pointing to his scar. 'She's got a bad temper but I know she doesn't mean it. She grew up in the streets. I get real deep in my raps, especially when I think about my sister. There's been a lot of struggling in my life and my lyrics are real. They're so real that I think that anyone can feel me, at anytime, whatever I'm saying.

'Right now the rap game is all about gold chains, cars and women and no one is saying nothing about real stuff. They scared to say something real on a record. Tupac was last person who said anything real. Nas – he's so real he won't get the credibility that others get. Nas don't break it down to the level where everyone can understand it though. I understand. I read a lot. I got some knowledge. But Nas has got to understand that there are people out there that don't understand what he's saying. These little boys in the ghetto that drop out of school in fifth or sixth grade ain't gonna think like that so he's gotta break it down to laymen's terms so everybody can understand.'

Heathon is as determined to make a change with his music as he is to change the climate for the hip hop scene in the city.

'People are scared of change and there's always one person scared to make that change,' he says. 'All of us right now have got to step up. There ain't nobody making it right now. We all just tell each other, "we doing this, we doing that. We just got to hook up with what's-her-name". Well let's all do what we gotta. Let's get this money. There's enough money out there for all of us. It ain't like the drugs man where there ain't enough money because – you know with the drug game how you get one person selling and they sell on this block, on that block. Everybody selling on every block and cutting each other's money so that's when the guns come in. Then we got to kill each other 'cos we're messing up each other's money. But it ain't like that in the rap game. I think we should just get out there and get things sorted, but it's like people are scared to get this money. I guess I'm scared too because I'm not making the sacrifices I need to do but you know the music, it's my life.'

Heathon could try leaving Chicago to make his mark. Others have done it. His music is good enough for labels outside of the city to take notice. His life in the city hasn't been easy. But, he says, Chicago is his heart. Like others in the city he feels the pulse of Chicago in his veins. Making music about life in the city and the city itself is his lifeblood. When he talks about Chicago it's like a man talking about a no-good lover he's hooked on.

'I love Chicago people. I love their humour. Don't matter how broke my crew is or whatever, we always gonna kick it and we're still going to be down for each other. Whatever they're doing all of the gang banging or whatever they doing we've still got love for one another. Even if we had jealousy on the rap and all that we still got love for each other. I feel like there's a lot of love but when it comes to making money, that's when things mess up. Like I say, I feel like money is the root of all evil. Nobody wants to see you with no more money that they've got. Like if I made it in Chicago I'd have to be careful where I live in the city. It's like me coming and eating in your face with a big old plate of food every day and I know you're starving. Pretty soon you're going to get pissed off and you going to take my plate of food. Not because you hate me but because you was hungry.'

Later that evening, back at my apartment, I was sitting on the porch, sipping a cold beer and listening to Heathon's song 'Black Rose' as I watched the sun dip behind the buildings across the way. The sound of wind chimes sparkled in the quiet night and fireflies were burning their flashes of green magic into the oncoming darkness as Heathon's quick-tongued rapping eased into the chorus of the song: 'Give me the beat so I can free my soul, black rose from the ground I grow, the fast life is the life I know, I want get lost in the rock and roll.'

If you want to get lost in music, then Chicago – with its live music venues, dance clubs, music bars, open mic sessions, concert halls and open-air events – seems like the perfect place to do it. Jazz fans, blues freaks, house heads and gospel devotees all make their pilgrimage to the city in the end. Every summer, thousands flock in on buses and planes, by car or by train to get their fix of the music they love, in its most organic, vibrant form. In Chicago you can see and hear artists perform any night of the week – whatever you want to hear and whatever you're into.

But for some of those struggling artists, music isn't just about enjoyment and fulfilment. For many Chicago artists, music is a means of understanding life and of making a living in a city that doesn't take any prisoners. For Heathon music is everything. Simple as that. Listen closely and within the sometimes soft, sometimes rasping lyrics that he tears from his gut, you'll hear a story of Chicago that doesn't get covered in magazines or newspaper articles on the city. It's rap music without fur coats and diamonds and with lyrics that sting without the bling. Listen to Heathon's words when he raps and you'll hear a story of a young black man's struggle to make the most of life in a tough, complex, hard-working city.

2 Jazz in the Wild Hundreds

I GOT TO experience the route down to the 'wild hundreds' first hand a few days later, when I was offered a ride to South Side jazz club, the New Apartment Lounge. I'd heard about this club, down south on 75th Street, but, as many had told a non-driver like me, 'it's the kind of place you need to get someone to take you to'. Getting a cab was another option but I was vociferously assured by anyone I'd spoken to on the matter that getting a cab back from 75th Street late at night would be neither safe nor easy. I got the same advice when I suggested taking the El to 75th and finding my way from there. I don't usually run my life according to what other people say; instead, I prefer to gather the evidence and make my own assumptions, but in the end it was something Duke said that made me change my mind.

'I don't mean to be personal but that ain't no neighbourhood for a white girl on her own to be headed at night,' he said.

'Oh,' I nodded.

'Can I speak bluntly?' Duke said slowly, fixing me with his sharp, old eyes.

'Go ahead.'

'Now Chicago's supposed to be an integrated city, that's what they say, but you stay in the city for long and you'll see that it's about as divided as it can be,' he said.

'How do you mean?'

'Well maybe I'm just speaking general here, or from my point of view. But the way I see it you got black folks living in the South, white folks in the North and Hispanics, blacks and Europeans in the West of the city and that just seems to be the way that it is.'

'I see.'

'Well that ain't no mind but if a white girl like you goes, all on her own, way down South Side late at night, well I think you could be looking at trouble.'

I'd only just arrived in town at the time and was determined to reserve judgement on the layout of the city until I'd had time to check it out myself but there was something about Duke that just made me take notice of what he said. Maybe it was to do with the fact that he didn't usually say much at all – so if he opened his mouth to speak, it had to be worth saying. Or maybe it was because if you carefully studied the lines on his face – like you would the lines on the inside of a tree if you cut it straight across the trunk – what you saw was a carefully etched map of a hard-worked, long-lived life of experience. I might not have known Duke well, or even at all when I came to think about it, but what he said got right to me. That's why when I was offered the chance to go down to 75th Street with someone who made regular business of going down there to the New Apartment Lounge on a Tuesday night, I jumped at the chance.

My escort, it turned out, was a guy named Mike Friedman, the owner of Chicago record label Premonition Records. I knew Premonition because I already owned records they had released by Terry Callier, a Chicago-based jazz/folk singer from the city who's been making music since the late 1960s, and by Chicago's own, hard bop, tenor sax legend Von Freeman. Premonition is the only label to have secured a joint imprint deal with the great Blue Note records. That's pretty good going by any means, especially when you're talking about a small, Chicago-based independent. So, like the name suggested, I had a feeling about this label when I called their office.

'Hi, is Mike there?' I asked the guy who picked up the phone.

'This is Mike,' he answered.

'Well, I've been a fan of your label for a while and I just recently got into town and would love to come by your office and meet you if that's okay.'

'Sure.'

'Sure?'

'Sure,' he said. 'Come by about 3pm if you like.'

The Premonition office is in Bucktown, one stop on the El from where I lived. Take the blue line from Division to Damon, he'd said, and you'll find it. So I did and I met Mike and, being the man who's released Von Freeman's last two albums, he offered to take me down to Von's regular session at the New Apartment Lounge.

'It's the quintessential Chicago place,' said Mike in the car on the way south that evening. 'It's been there for 50 years or so and at one point it was one of the big jazz rooms in the country. Gene Ammons played there. Sonny Stitt played there and Charlie Parker did too. There are three rooms in the club and on Tuesday nights the small one becomes the jazz room and that's where Von plays. It's a corner, neighbourhood bar, not a music room and there's no cover charge. You just go there and it's pure music. That's all it is and Von's been doing the Tuesday nights there since 1980. Von's quartet plays the first hour. They usually play like an hour and a half set. Then it's opened up for a jam session until 3.30am. At midnight you get kids streaming in to play. It's the best jazz session in Chicago. It's a great destination for people. It's kind of in the heart of the ghetto and you know what, I don't think it's changed since he started doing it.'

Despite the fact he must be pushing 40, when Mike speaks about something he likes he turns into a teenager, delivering each sentence with a smile that's like sunshine. His bright, dark eyes sparkle behind a smart pair of glasses with black rims that match his short-cropped, sooty hair and pointy beard. In the flat, rectangular, lenses of his specs, I catch the glimmer of the streetlights as his focus flicks between my face and the road. From my place in Wicker Park, we drive the 'scenic route' through downtown and across to South Wabash in the heart of the South Loop. In the late part of the 19th century, this area between 18th and 22nd Streets and running out west as far as Wentworth Avenue was Chicago's red-light district, known back then as the Levee. The 44,000 black people who lived then in Chicago were packed into the South Side between 16th and 39th Streets and it was here that the city's nightlife blossomed.

We pause in traffic on Wabash and as Mike chatters, I scour this patch of road and cross streets for a hint of those hedonistic days gone by. On my right there's a run-down Thai restaurant, a scruffy bookstore and a grocery mart; on my left a busy multi-storey parking lot. Buses and cars inch across the street in front of us and all around Chicago folk go about their Tuesday night business, but nowhere are there any clues to what this area would have been like a hundred years ago. Written in the much-scribed history of jazz are tales of how pianist Scott Joplin would hang out in the bawdy piano bars dotted between the 260 licensed prostitution dens in this cross-section of streets in the mid-1890s to hear local, in-house piano players Arthur Marshall and Louis Chavin. It was their upbeat, jaunty, bar-room music that was a big influence for Joplin, who moved to Chicago in 1894 and worked in those self-same piano bars banging out peppy numbers every night of the week in pre-Prohibition times.

Joplin's 'The Entertainer' might be the world's best-known ragtime piano tune but it was his 1899-penned, revised version of his own 'Maple Leaf Rag' that was a bigger hit in the city at the time. At the turn of the century, it was this piece that could be heard blaring out of whorehouses and bars up and down the city's now very stately State Street. The bars and whorehouses may be gone now, but the legacy of those early ragtime pieces, played by Marshall, Chavin, Joplin and other pianists around the city, lie at the very roots of jazz music as we know it today. Joplin himself was a big influence on New Orleans piano man Jelly Roll Morton who spent a lot of time in Chicago in the early part of the 20th century and blazed a trail between ragtime and jazz.

Jazz might not have been born in Chicago but it was here that King Oliver recorded 'King Porter Stomp', one of the early jazz tunes first set down for posterity in 1924. But Oliver had been playing in the city way before then: his Creole Jazz Band was actually the first jazz band to play live in Chicago in 1912. There's not much record of the band being in town because they played on the South Side, and so few people knew about it. They didn't record back then either. Later it was claimed that a white band from New Orleans called the Original Dixieland Jass Band were the first to play in the city in 1914. This band – made up of Nick LaRocca, Eddie Edwards, Larry Shields, Henry Ragas and Tony Sbarabro – was the first jazz band to set their music to record with their 'Barnyard Blues' out in 1917 on Victor. They weren't the most exciting band of the time, but because no one else was recording during this period they became more popular than other bands that were around in the city. Recording didn't start in Chicago until Brunswick – the commercial record company also known for making bowling balls – opened a studio in the city in 1921. The ten-year period after Brunswick opened marked the most exciting era for the city's jazz scene, despite the political circumstances of the time. In January 1920, the National Prohibition Act was put into effect, outlawing the importation, exportation, transportation, sale and manufacture of alcohol. Although this law initially seemed set to ruin the local bars and taverns in the city, what it succeeded in doing instead was to drive the drinking dens, which were fuelled by music and dancing, underground. It was during this time that jazz music in the city flourished. Cornettists Louis Armstrong and Bix Beiderbecke, clarinettist Benny Goodman and drummer Gene Krupa were all around during this time, playing and recording regularly in the city. Between them, they unwittingly set up the framework for a 'Chicago style' of jazz music, building on the rhythmic permutations of the New Orleans pioneers and the big band euphoria and adding to this a burst of urban energy and intensity.

Later on – in the wake of this era and post-prohibition – Oliver's 'King Porter Stomp' was made popular in the city by jazzman Benny Goodman, who played a 1936-penned Fletcher Henderson arrangement of it. At that time, Von Freeman would have been just 14 years old.

'Von's really the dean,' says Mike, excitedly, as he pulls away from the shifting line of traffic. 'He's the best jazz musician that we have in Chicago. He's 80 years old, so he's a living history of jazz. He was born in 1922, so he was born pretty much when it was incubating and lived through incredible times of the music's history. In the 1920s and 1930s

esided in Chicago and he caught a glimmer of that when
a kid. In the 1940s, there was an incredible local music
cially in jazz but also in the blues – and all that stuff kind
of developed around that time.'

Past 22nd Street, Mike chats away and as the blocks slip by slowly,
the moonlit roads outside turn from downtown gaudiness into well-
worn, urban sprawl. Behind us the towering silver and glass of
Chicago's skyline is like a distant fairytale castle, luminous against the
inky sky; and all the while we're heading further away from it, driving
deeper south. As we dip past the quiet warehouses on 45th and 46th
Streets, it seems there's fewer people about. Although darkness hides
the details, in the soft, yellow glow of the streetlamps I can just make
out the good neighbourhoods from the bad. As the streets descend, I
notice the suit shops, nail parlours and mobile phone stores that line
them boarded up for the night, with only furtive signs of life outside
chicken stops and corner liquor stores. We pause at a traffic light and
on the corner, to my right, a group of men and women hang; they are
drinking out of half-pint bottles in brown paper bags and chatting in
the gentle night breeze. Two men sit on low stools outside a storefront,
shooting dice at the side of the building. I look a few hundred yards
back down the street to where a pig-ear sandwich truck is parked with
a bored-looking man tending it. The sides of the truck are opened up
like wings and a sign reading 'bread, pig ears and hot sauce sandwich
$3' hangs from a chain down the side of the truck.

At a stop sign in the bowl of a valley of four looming tower blocks,
a group of men and boys are gathered round a blazing oil drum. The
edges of the rusty drum are fluid in the fervour of the fire and, in the
balmy summer's night air it must be excitement and not heat that the
onlookers are seeking in the rampant flames. As we pull away, one of
the men raises his arm and motions to the car but his words are lost as
we drive on. Minutes later we pause again to let a woman as wide as
a bus with jeans that are more holes than denim cross the street; she is
cussing the skinny-hipped, round-shouldered, despondent male
walking two steps behind her. Her spiky, chaffing words are like short,
sharp punches to his stickman frame; each delivered with tosses of her

head. We drive on again and her staccato shrieks momentarily break
the steady rhythm of Mike's words.

Mike started Premonition in 1993. He'd moved to Chicago in 1980
and, as a hopeful young jazz drummer, was out to find work in the city.
He had heard about Von's Tuesday jazz session, so he went down to
the New Apartment Lounge hoping for a break.

'That's pretty much what you have to do,' he says. 'You have to go
down there and play with the man. Even back then, he was the best so
I went down there to play. He doesn't remember me from back then at
all. After that I hung around the city for a while getting into this and
that; then I kind of drifted around. I moved to New York for a bit.
Came back here and then started the record company. It wasn't until I
got the Blue Note contract into place in 2000 that I came across this
guy who said to me: "I've got this tape of Von Freeman from a gig up
in Minneapolis. The record company is closing down and doesn't
know what to do with it." I heard the tape and bought it. It was a
session called "Live At The Dakota". I got in touch with Von and he
was into the idea so we put it out. It worked well. We really enjoyed
working together so we did another one last year called "The
Improvisor" and we've already got another one in the can ready for
release.

'It's been great. Von's really what I enjoy in music. He's an
individual. He doesn't copy anyone else. His approach to music is that
you have to have your own thing, your own style, which is really what
jazz music is all about as far as I'm concerned. I don't think playing
jazz in clubs was ever very lucrative and it has never been weighed
towards financial security. Having a recording career was the route to
an artist getting better gigs and more money but those sorts of deals
have been few and far between in the jazz world, compared to how
many people made records. I just think people play music for the
reason they have to play music. That's what it's all about and that's
what it's about with Von. He's never had any other job. He's been poor
but he's always done his thing and expressed himself. That's how jazz
keeps getting reinvented every ten years and that's all down to people
like Von who push the envelope of what people accept as what the

music should be. Music is all about constantly changing as individuals, searching out your own individual expression and Von still lives that. That's what I love about music and there's a lot of that here in Chicago. That's what I think will save us in the end, if we're meant to be saved.

'There's certain places that are music places – where music is in people's blood – and Chicago is one of them. I'm not sure why that is, but when the wind chill factor is 30 degrees below in the middle of January and you go into a club and it's packed, you just know that music is important to people. You know that it's part of their lives. I've been to other places and it's just not like that but for some reason it means something to Chicago people. That all this music is happening around them. I think there's just something about being in the middle of the country. Being in the heartland, which is where you are when you are here. Don't even think that Chicago is anything bigger than the capital of the Mid West though, because that's just what it is. It reflects the people that grew up in the Mid West and, going back to the early 20th century, people from down South. In the first half of the 20th century, Mississippi practically emptied out and ended up in the South Side of Chicago. That's an interesting thing about Chicago too that makes it a really wonderful place – and you'll see that in the New Apartment tonight.'

It might be dark outside but around the pale blue, formica, M-shaped bar that fills the middle of the small, dimly lit, smoky jazz room of the New Apartment Lounge sit at least half a dozen men, nursing drinks and wearing shades. But this is no college crowd or collection of downtown trendies because these men in this bar look like they could have been sitting here, holding those same drinks and wearing those same shades, since the Sixties. Behind the bar, a bony wisp of a woman with a shrivelled face as sour as if she's been sucking lemons is moving fluidly between the dozen or so customers waiting to be served. Her small, wiry hands manipulate bottles, handfuls of money, spent glasses, mixers and cascading ice cubes with the dexterity of Tom Cruise in the 1980s movie *Cocktail*. Her wizened face looks old but it's hard to judge exactly how many years she's stacked up. Either she's been tending this bar since it opened in 1953 or she's just had some tough customers to deal with recently. Either way, if ever there was a bartender born to tend bars, then this is the one. An old-style cash till with raised bell-buttons and a tray reaching the tender's chin sits in the middle of a counter behind the bar, the length of it backed by a long mirror that runs up to the low ceiling. Reflected in it are bottles of wines, spirits, cordials, bourbons and mixers, wedged onto the counter and packing the space around the till. Behind the reflection of the legion of bottles are the mirror-faces of the men waiting patiently to be served.

I soon work out that the bartender is called Weezie. 'Short for Louise,' a man sitting next to me whispers, his eyes flicking nervously between my face and Weezie herself, making sure she hasn't heard him as she moves slowly but solidly between customers. There's people waiting to be served and, the longer I sit at the bar, the more I realise that getting a drink in the New Apartment Lounge is no swift process. Most of the men waiting for drinks are three times the size of Weezie but not one of them tries to hurry her along. In this small neighbourhood bar, deep in the South Side of Chicago, on a Tuesday night, you get the feeling that this little sour-faced lady is very much in charge. So composed is she in her task of managing the bar that when the man of the night, Von Freeman himself, strolls in looking dapper in a tight blue t-shirt, smart black trousers and with his snowy hair perfectly coiffed, she barely flicks her eyes up from her task.

'If I were 79 years old you know there'd be trouble for a pretty little fox like you,' smiles 80-year-old Von, nursing his beer at the deserted bar out back where, at Mike's suggestion, I've ushered him for a pre-gig chat. It's this part smooth-talking hep-cat, part jovial old charmer that I had expected to find but the real deal – Vonski in action – is even more than I could have hoped for. It was 11pm when he walked in. With just ten minutes left till he's due to play, I've got him to myself. For a man who was born in 1922 and has been playing music for nearly all those years since, you might expect Von to be slightly worn out or a little bit jaded. But this living legend is lively as someone a third his age, and as approachable and friendly as anyone can be.

'I was supposed to be a conductor but the jazz got hold of me and I couldn't do anything but play that jazz. The jazz got me. It still got me,' smiles Von. 'I'm an improvisor so I live to express myself. Sometimes it sounds alright and sometimes it's kind of weird but that's the way I feel. I play the way I feel.'

Von plays 'hardcore jazz', he says, a sound that was born and nurtured in the city when Von was growing up. It's a form he has built on and adapted over the years, and a style of playing that has seen him through the changing faces of music in the city.

'Well, you know, I think it's a Chicago thing,' he says. 'Every musician from this city, whatever instrument they seem to play, they have a kind of growl in what they're playing. I've used the term "hardcore jazz" to describe the music that comes out of Chicago before and I don't know why it fits so well but it just does. Maybe it's something to do with the fact that Chicago is a hard place or maybe it's from some kind of discontent we all got here but that hardness comes out in the music.

'You know I learned music the hard way too, without much instruction. Like most poor cats, you just finally come up with an instrument of some kind and you teach yourself, which is bad really because you really should get instruction. Otherwise you just learn a lot of stuff you've got to decode later on in life. Somewhere along the line, if you're going to be at all good, you have to finally end up taking lessons and you got to do that with a decent instrument, not a tired old beat-up horn.'

There are thousands of stories that come out of any city but if we're talking about jazz stories, and we're talking about Chicago, then one of my favourites has got to be the one about how Von got his first horn. He's told the story a million times, in a million different ways. But when I finally have the man himself sitting there, large 'as life on a stool in front of me, I want to hear the story first hand.

'See the Victrola,' he begins, 'that's an instrument that plays records and my father, he was a great lover of music, he had a Victrola and that was kind of a prize during those times. Only well-to-do folk had

Victrolas but my father, somehow, he had got one. He had some of these old, heavy, wax records he'd play on that machine and you had to wind it up to play them and I was the winder. Now I might have only been six years old at the time but I was already into music. We had a piano in our house and as soon as I could get up on that stool I was banging away on that piano but the thing I really loved was the saxophone. I would listen to my father's records by horn blowers from that era, like Louis Armstrong and Rudy Vallee, and I would be looking in books to find out about the saxophone. I wanted to see pictures of it and see how it worked. So anyway one day, I was winding up that Victrola and it struck me that this thing had a head that was shaped just something like a saxophone. So what I did was I waited till my father was out and I took his prize instrument, removed the big bell, bore holes in it, attached a mouth piece and made me a saxophone.'

His father, says Von, was 'disgusted' but rather than chide his boy his reaction when he'd cooled down, Von remembers, was: 'Oh Lord, let's get this boy some kind of horn.' Von's father was a well-connected jazz fan. He brought Louis Armstrong round to the house when Von was just a boy. The music and his upbringing had a strong impact on Von. Initially he taught himself to play his horn but later on Von took lessons from the legendary Chicago music teacher Captain Walter Dyett, who taught at the Du Sable High School.

'I finally went to school and finally got instruction,' remembers Von. 'But before that, like I said, I was just the average young guy in the ghetto trying to make my way with music. You just fake it. I'm still faking it. That's the way I came up. I was lucky enough to join Horace Henderson, that's Fletcher Henderson's brother, in his band playing at the Rhumboogie.'

The Rhumboogie Club, owned by local entrepreneur Joe Louis, was on 343 East Garfield Street at 55th South, just south of King Drive which, back then, was South Parkway. It was here, at this show lounge, that Von, at the tender age of seventeen, joined Horace Henderson's big band. The Rhumboogie was, at that time, one of the most popular clubs in the city and when Horace let the word out that he needed a tenor sax player, Von was recommended for the job. He was still in school at the time and had landed a college scholarship to play first clarinet but he jacked in the role to take up in Henderson's band at the Rhumboogie.

'Horace's big band was very popular, very hip. He was the one that really trained me into the big time. All these guys were big pros. They were calling me young blood and they pulled tricks on me every night. I wore my daddy's tuxedo and they thought that was really funny. I came in there with this old-fashioned tuxedo on 'cos I didn't have no money for no tuxedo and I'd never even played in one.'

Every evening at the Rhumboogie, back in those days, was the same. The show would start with a big introduction from the band, during which time the 'Rhumboogie Girls' would come out, dance 'The Middle Number' and parade around the floor. Then the girls would go off, the band – set in a pit down by the front of the stage – would play some more and a comedian, a tap dancer and a singer would come on. This was the height of the swing era. Swing, as the new form of jazz, was characterised by very large bands and fixed arrangements and it emerged during the 1930s as an adaptation of the commercially successful but bland neo-jazz played by show and dance orchestras. In the hands of brilliant arrangers like Fletcher Henderson, however, swing combined harmonic sophistication with danceable rhythms and compelling individual improvisations. Just like the Rhumboogie, it was the same drill that would happen in the other show lounges that were around in the city at that time: the DeLisa, the Ritz and the Grand Terrace. But it was here, at the Rhumboogie, that Von cut his 'big time' teeth.

'Consequently time went on and I was inducted into the navy where I played in the great navy band The Hellcats,' recalls Von. 'This band was shipped out to Hawaii so I spent my time over there with all those lovely Hawaiian ladies. When the war was over I made it back here and I've been struggling along playing ever since.'

Post-war Chicago was a sombre place, with little money around and people struggling to get by. Despite these difficult times, music in the city flourished, with musicians travelling in from all over America to make the most of the accessibility of Chicago's music scene. During the mid to late 1930s, the swing bands had been big in the major cities in America and you could hear their live broadcasts regularly on the radio. By the time World War Two hit, swing music had been around for a while. Many of the musicians were drafted into the army and a gap was left for a new style of music to come in. Younger players took the place of the musicians who had gone to fight in the war and with them they brought a darker, meatier element into the jazz music of the time. Instruments like the clarinet and sax were better suited to this sound and eventually they usurped the popularity of the trumpet, the instrument that had ruled swing. The new sound, labelled 'bebop', was popularised at the time by musicians like Dizzy Gillespie, Charlie Parker and Billy Eckstein.

By the time the Second World War ended, the shift was decisive. The war, however, had taken its toll on the economy and the big swing bands were forced to split. Even big band leader Count Basie, a regular visitor to Chicago, had a sextet by then. With the exception of Dizzy Gillespie and Billy Eckstein's two big bands, the post-war bebop jazz sound was mostly made up of trios and quartets.

The big show lounges of Chicago suffered during these times and the city's jazz music scene decamped from the big-scale lounges into smaller taverns and bars around Chicago.

'The taverns more or less took over,' remembers Von. 'There was three and four in every block; sometimes more than that and a lot of the smaller combos and duos would play at those. Some taverns operated just like piano lounges with just a piano player and a singer.'

Jazz music began to lose its big stars and to focus on smaller groups and it was these ensembles that Von remembers seeing a lot of in Chicago. People like John Coltrane, Charlie Parker, Sonny Rollins, Johnny Griffin, Lockjaw Davis, James Moody and Dizzy would all make it to the city to play and Von would go and see them as often as he could. Later on, when the economy picked up again, Von landed a gig playing in the basement at the Pershing Hotel on 64th and Cottage Grove. Von knew the guy who did bookings at the hotel and when his three-month stint ended, he was offered the band slot in the hotel's ballroom. Joined by his brothers George and Bruz, Von backed greats like Dizzy, Billie Holiday and Charlie Parker. The Pershing Ballroom was half a block long and a block wide and attracted people from all over the city and out of town and, for a few years, was one of the jazz hotspots in Chicago. It wasn't until Charlie Parker died in 1955 that the crowd at the Pershing started thinning out. Von's gig eventually ended; his brothers moved to New York to find work and Von himself married, had children, and continued to play around the city. By then the musical tide in Chicago was already shifting and the first strains of a new musical movement, known back then as R&B, were starting to grip the city.

'I really got to hit,' says Von, picking up his horn and walking back into the small bar. I follow him through and pull up the same stool I'd been sitting at before and watch him get ready to play. He slowly opens his case, takes out his sax and tools up. From a pocket in the side of a small, black bag he pulls out a pair of large, black sunglasses and puts them on. He leans up against the CD juke box sitting in front of the right-hand side of the stage and, with his back flat against its side and his left foot resting up on the stage, he nods at the drummer to begin. The drummer yields with a gentle rhythm and the bass player plucks a simple b-line. Von's head is hung as if in meditation while the guitar player joins in and then, just as the atmosphere in the small room warms and the crowd has started toe-tapping to the music, Von blows from his sax. The crowd claps to herald his first few notes and then it slips into the mood.

As the atmosphere inside the New Apartment Lounge is soothed by the cool music, on the street outside, two old guys with hangdog faces peer into the club. In the glow of the flickering streetlamp, a girl walks across the road and into the liquor store on the opposite corner. One of the old hangdogs slides into the bar and stands with his back against the wall while Von plays. The only seats in the room are stools around the M-shaped bar and by the time Von starts these are full. Halfway through the band's first number, the first of the evening's hopefuls turns up, a skinny kid who can't be more than 20 years old. He shuffles into the room holding his guitar case under one arm and mopping the beads of sweat on his forehead with his other free hand. He finds a spot and stands, back against the wall, waiting patiently for his turn to play with the great.

I'm dry-throated from the hot night. 'I'll have a beer,' I say to Weezie.

The dark, tight, stay-wet curls that cling to her thin face frame a frown so ferocious, set firm in spite of the cool music, that I'm convinced this can only be a stern act, hiding a soppy interior. Determined to prove myself right, I fix Weezie with my biggest, widest grin in an attempt to crack the crone.

'You got to stop smiling and start telling me which beer you want, lady,' she snaps.

'Erm, Budweiser,' I stutter.

Weezie stares coldly back at me, then shakes her head in disapproval and moves slowly over to the under-the-counter fridge at the far end of the small bar.

'You know she keeps a baseball bat behind the bar,' says a voice from the stool next to me. I look up slowly to my left and see an old man in a blue suit, white shirt and thin blue tie wearing a dark blue trilby hat with a black felt trim that's perched sideways on his head. I recognise him as the same man who'd whispered Weezie's real name to me earlier on. His gangly legs hang with his feet hitting the floor and his long, thin arms are resting on the formica bar top.

'You seen her use it?' I ask.

'Two or three times,' he says with a broad grin that reveals more gummy gaps than teeth.

His name, it turns out, is John and he's been drinking in bars around 75th street since the 1960s. He's always lived around here, he tells me, and he's been coming to Von's night at the New Apartment Lounge every Tuesday since as long as he can remember.

Mike, who's been absent since we entered the New Apartment, re-appears from a murky back room of the club and comes over to where John and I are sitting. It seems that Mike knows this smart-dressed, friendly man who must be pushing 80 if he's a day. While they chat about what kind of week they've had, I look around me. On the tiny stage by the door, Von's band is doing its thing, unamplified, but with enough volume to guide the mood in the bar. Jack Zara on bass stands in the left corner, eyes closed, sweat pouring from his brow, plucking rhythmically at his instrument; Michael Raynor on drums is positioned to the right, feather-stroking his cymbals; between the two of them, they take up the whole of the cosy stage. In front of Michael, Mike Allemana on guitar is poised on a chair, head down, in deep concentration, fiddling with his frets and waiting for the right time to join in. Opposite him is Von, doing his 'outside' stuff to the band's music. Von plays the melody of 'What Is This Thing Called Love' and the atmosphere lifts. Then the band breaks it back down and a mesmeric, heart-stopping drum solo ensues, shifting the mood again.

The sonic story goes on until past midnight and the long, wide window that takes up the whole of the wall behind the stage shows a dark, empty street outside, strobe-lit with the flicker of the gloomy streetlamp. In 2003, that same street was named 'Von Freeman Boulevard' after the man himself. As part of a tribute to the jazzman and to tie in with his 80th birthday, the city awarded him an honorary doctorate from Northwestern University and his very own street. It's an old habit in Chicago and that's how the long stretch of road known as Parkway, running from downtown right into the heart of the South Side of the city, became Martin Luther King Drive. So on Von's street, at Von's own jazz session, numbers are swelling in the bijou New Apartment Lounge. It's a motley bunch that makes up the crowd in the Apartment and though the average age of customer is at least 55 years old, this is no old-timers tea party. Dudes in sharp suits mingle with cats in Kangol hats and 1980s Tacchini sports jackets and jittery, strung-out, street-stalkers. It might be a different story in other cities but here, on Chicago's South Side, the septuagenarian drill come 11 o'clock is to reach for your Brylcreem, buff up your hair, grab a pair of sunglasses and head down to the New Apartment Lounge.

Weezie mooches back over with my beer and slaps it down on the counter. I nervously hand her a five-dollar bill and patiently wait for my change. She moves over to the till, punches a few buttons, opens the tray, stashes the five-dollar bill, pulls out two notes and some coins and heads back over, ignoring my outstretched palm and dumping the contents of her bony hand down next to my beer. I swallow hard and reach for my bottle just as Weezie pulls a tall glass of Coke from underneath the counter, takes a swig and plonks it down by the wall in front of John.

'Keep your eyes on it and your lips off it,' Weezie barks.

'It's yours, baby,' John replies. His hands are up in the air, in surrender position. Weezie raises her eyebrows and moves towards another customer as John turns to me.

'She mean,' he smiles, shaking his head.

The minutes slip by and the New Apartment Lounge gets fuller with the space around the bar soon three deep and the queue of hopefuls – guitarists, keyboardists, trumpet players, bassists – growing until it spills out onto the street. The crowd get rowdier as Von's band play their signature 'hardcore jazz' and between bursts, the 80-year-old master, back against the juke box, shades on, one foot up on stage, shuts his eyes and selects the moments to play. The band's take on standards is supplemented by Von's own take on familiar melodies and each time he comes in, the crowd responds with a murmuring applause. As midnight slides into the smaller hours, the room adopts that 'in between time' feeling that Duke Ellington collaborator Billy Strayhorn would so often talk about. It's at those in between times, Strayhorn used to say, not quite night and not quite morning, when anything can happen and anything is possible. It's only during that time of day when you can say what you like and do what you like and none of it matters. I don't know how many beers I had that night, or how many hopefuls got up on that stage to play with Von. I can't remember to whom I spoke or if I only imagined that Weezie actually showed me the beginnings of a smile. I do remember that, by the time Mike managed to drag me off my bar stool to head home, it was something that Von had said earlier that rang in my ears. 'I really think good jazz is good for your health,' he had told me, just before he was about to take the stage. The image of that 80-year-old man, still blowing his horn as we left the New Apartment Lounge that night, left me in no doubt that he was right.

3 Velvet Room Jazz

IT WAS while tucking into a bowl of curly sweet potato fries in Hilary's Urban Eatery, on the north corner of my street and Division, that I thought about another of the city's tenor sax players. I drank Diet Coke out of a large jam jar, which is just the way they serve all the drinks in there, and found my mind wandering towards Fred Anderson. It was Saturday afternoon and outside the traffic was hissing angrily in a jam stretching all the way from downtown as far up Division as I could see from my window seat. From the air-conditioned haven of Hilary's, I chewed on the sweet, warm saltiness of the curly fry and watched a group of kids hanging out on the corner, chatting in the searing midday heat. A mutt wandered past the group, red-eyed and slow in the hot sun, then stopped in a small pool of shade right by the newspaper stand. The dog lazily lifted a leg and shot out a hot stream against the side of the paper stand, then slowly slouched off into the sunshine.

Inside the restaurant, as noon slipped into afternoon and the tables started filling with the weekend lunch crowd, I thought about the stories I'd heard about the 74-year-old Fred Anderson. I'd seen pictures of him playing his sax on the tiny stage of his jazz watering hole the Velvet Lounge, on the near South Side of the city. In those frozen shots taken in front of the faded, multi-coloured, flowers-and-stripes Seventies wallpaper, I'd got a picture-image of Anderson as he looks today: small, bespectacled, sweet, always wearing a hat over his close-cut, salt and pepper hair. I'd shared my image of this horn blower with a fellow from the city's Jazz Institute I'd met at a gig once and he just laughed and said that's what a lot of people who don't really know Fred say about him. I asked him how he'd describe Fred and he said the seasoned sax player was more like a 'virile Buddha' to him. It was a description that intrigued me, almost as much as all the other stories I'd heard about Anderson since I'd arrived in the city.

A sax player since he was a teenager, Anderson learned to play during the 1940s bebop era when jazz artists like Charlie Parker and John Coltrane were striking out with their unique take on the form. It was Parker's concept of sound that became Anderson's musical raison d'être.

Parker came through in the 1940s and it was his innovation of improvising a new melody line from the top, rather than the middle of the informing chord, that provided a new slant on the jazz sound that had dominated the previous decade. The harmonious superiority of Parker's sound, along with the equally sonorous style purveyed by musicians like Dizzy Gillespie and Thelonious Monk, went part of the way to defining the bebop sound of the 1940s.

But Parker's definition ran even deeper than that. He saw music as a journey, with a multitude of different avenues. By playing music, you could go wherever you wanted to go, wherever your subconscious mind told you to go. This meditative approach to music was something that set Parker apart from his contemporaries. He believed that, with musical creativity, it was within your subconscious mind that everything happened. Your subconscious is restoring itself with sounds every day, he would say, and that's where improvisation comes in. Parker believed in always having some direction to go musically, never allowing yourself to get trapped in a corner. And if you did find yourself trapped, he believed, you could always figure out how to escape. Like life, music for Parker was about situations and solutions.

It was Parker's style and ideas about sound that Fred heard and learned from on recordings and at live gigs he caught around the city when he was growing up. From those early days of listening to Parker, Coltrane and Lester Young play, Fred determined to make his own musical way through life. Anderson is now one of Chicago's best living tenor saxophonists and, like other seasoned horn players like Von

Freeman, he has lived and worked in the city all his life and stuck to his guns musically. Unlike Freeman, Anderson has worked other jobs as a means of supporting his family but has always managed to keep the music going.

Back in the Sixties and early Seventies, when Anderson made his first recordings, the city was just reclaiming its jazz roots and a new strain of avant garde jazz music was moving across Chicago. In the late Seventies, Fred ran a club near his home, northwest of the city in Evanston. The club was called Birdhouse and was named after his idol Charlie Parker. Fred would present up and coming jazz artists from the city at this club and it was after being spotted by an Austrian pianist called Dieter Glawishnig, who was touring the US, that he bagged a tour of Europe as part of Dieter's Neighbours trio. During this tour Fred recorded his first album with the Neighbours: *Accents* which was released on MRC's Electoral label.

After that tour Fred headed to Europe again, taking his quintet with him. Fred's ensemble played at the Seventh International New Jazz Festival in Moers, Germany. Some of his compositions were recorded live at that festival and released as a long-player called *Another Day* on Moers Music. That was the late Seventies. Previous to that, Fred had been innovating back home via his work with the Chicago-spawned jazz collective the Association For The Advancement of Creative Musicians (AACM).

The AACM was formed in the mid-Sixties and comprised a collection of musicians and composers who wanted to redefine ways of presenting new and challenging avant garde jazz music. They would meet in each other's homes and would organise concerts and events that strayed outside of the city's club scene; and they frequently played in churches, community centres and theatres around the city. With AACM members Joseph Jarman on reeds, Bill Brimfield on trumpet, Charles Clark on bass, and Arthur Reed on drums, Fred played his sax for the first ever AACM gig on 71st Street in 1964. In the 1980s he transformed a dingy watering hole on 2128 1/2 S Indiana, that had been in existence since the 1970s, into the Velvet Lounge, a corner stone for freeform, dissonant jazz music in the city.

The Velvet Lounge is in a part of town called Bronzeville, a once thriving, African-American neighbourhood that, back in the early part of the 20th century, incorporated jazz hotbed The Stroll. Now the 'Gateway To Bronzeville' on Martin Luther King Jr Drive is marked by a 15-foot-tall statue called the 'Monument To The Great Northern Migration'. The bronze statue, which dominates the middle of the street, depicts an African-American man, wearing a suit and hat and walking. He carries a suitcase in one hand and he waves with the other – a farewell to the South, or a greeting to Chicago, or both. The 1.5-mile 'Walk Of Fame' that runs from this point, between 25th and 47th Streets on Martin Luther King Drive, cuts through the heart of a long-forgotten neighbourhood. The area's vibrant past is commemorated in some 91 plaques marking the significant characters who once lived or worked here. Louis Armstrong is one of them; and crooner Nat King Cole is commended along this stretch.

In past years, Bronzeville as a historical site was ignored by the city and little money was invested in preserving it. Important buildings were knocked down, memorials left untended. The area, which once possessed the atmosphere of New York's Harlem, has in recent years had to rely on its own residents for support. Yet, despite community efforts, many of the Bronzeville taverns and clubs that defined the area's music scene have closed down. The Velvet Lounge is one of the few remaining.

It's the same today as it was when Fred Anderson took it over in 1980. Like most old-style Chicago taverns, it's not much more than a corridor with a long bar and an opening at the end just big enough to fit a few tables and a small stage. Unassuming it might be but this venue has, over the years, played host to jazz players from the city and beyond. AACM founder Ari Brown plays regularly down there. On Sundays, the open jam session works as a platform for young jazz players in the city who want to try out their skills. In the late 1990s, the Sunday night session got so busy that Fred had to set up a Wednesday night jam session just to give more chance for young jazz players to perform. Like Freeman's Tuesday nights at the New Apartment Lounge, Anderson's Velvet Lounge remains an unsung institution in the city.

Fred's commitment to free jazz was first put on record in *Song For*, by a group led by Joseph Jarman and released on Delmark in 1966. In recent years Anderson has done a spate of recordings on the local Okka Disc label, which was set up specifically to release his music. This output has brought him more attention and accolades than he has ever previously received. And by all accounts, he certainly deserves it.

I'd heard Anderson's recordings before arriving in the city. Through books, magazines and hearsay, I'd slowly pieced together a patchwork tale of this tenor sax man's life, ad libbing from my own imagination as you do when you ponder the life and story of anyone you admire from afar. Facts provide a framework of a person's existence, what their life has been like and who they really are and, set against a backdrop of the city of Chicago, my picture of Fred Anderson was one that tied in with the history of avant garde jazz music in the city. But it was the stories about Fred himself, the ones that I'd picked up since arriving in Chicago, that brought flourishes of colour and shades of light and dark to the detailed line drawing I'd mentally created of this man.

I soon found out that if I mentioned Fred Anderson's name to pretty much any jazz fan in the city they had a ready-to-tell story about him. A few simply described him as a 'sweetheart'. Some told how he'd 'brought up' many jazz musicians in the city and given them a platform to perform that had enriched their careers – like the drummer Hamid Drake who first played with Fred at a jam session down at the Velvet Lounge and still plays and records with him today. Others described how Fred had worked many years at a local rug company to earn enough money to raise his family and yet still managed to keep up his music. Only a few knew that one of his two sons died recently in a motorcycle accident and that the other one has no burning interest in music, or in taking over the Velvet Lounge should anything happen to Fred. Most agreed, however, that whenever Fred picks up his horn, and starts blowing it, this small, sweet-looking old man turns into a strong, muscular powerhouse of a sax player, ageless and timeless and out there, somewhere, in a world of his own. Playing with the speed and grace of a master, moving up and down the scales with the agility of a sonic gymnast, Fred is his truest self when he's making music. It was time for my story of Fred Anderson.

By the time I'd finished the last of my curly sweet potato fries and my Diet Coke, the only thing left to do was to go and find him. And from what I could gather, the best place to find him was right there at the Velvet Lounge on a Saturday night.

'YOU'RE HERE really early you know,' said Fred, peering at me suspiciously through the half-opened door of the Velvet Lounge when I arrived there that night.

'I called you earlier,' I explained, smiling at this hobbit-like character who looked back at me with a face that gave nothing away.

'Oh, you better come in then,' conceded Fred, pulling back the door of the Lounge and showing me in.

Sitting next door to a fried chicken shop on a quiet, deserted street surrounded by warehouses, the Velvet Lounge could be easy to miss to the untrained eye. But if you hail down a cab anywhere in the city and ask them to take you to the Velvet Lounge they'll go straight there, without question. Cabs in the city are cheap and are air-conditioned, which in this early August heat is more than a blessing. Sometimes, though, just because I could imagine my mother tutting at the thought of me 'throwing money away', I would get a bus – and the day I went to the Velvet Lounge that's exactly what I did. The number 3 CTA bus goes south on Michigan from downtown towards Martin Luther King Jr Drive and if you stay on this bus until 14th Street, it'll drop you pretty much outside the Velvet Lounge. Stuck on the near South Side, there's no risk involved in getting a bus, although I'd been told that a cab back late at night from anywhere in the city was always a wise move.

Nearly all buses in Chicago are now also air-conditioned; a necessity in the city since a heatwave in July 1995 that killed nearly 700 people in the space of one week. On my way out of the hectic downtown area, breathing easily in the cool, temperature-regulated air, it struck me how well Chicago worked as a city. While some urban areas strain and heave under the weight of too many people, poor infrastructure and inadequate facilities, Chicago seemed to cope well. For sure, there were a lot of people about and endless streams of traffic dominated the main drags. All the same, though, it seemed to me that everything worked pretty well in this town.

So, when Fred Anderson opened the door of the Velvet Lounge that afternoon, I was feeling cooled and calmed from my easy bus ride. Certainly, I little expected what I found inside his club.

Almost as soon as you walk into the Velvet Lounge and the door shuts behind you, the place absorbs you and you immediately feel at home. Peeling paint on the ceilings, nicotine-stained papered walls, pictures of past jazz masters on the walls and fixtures and fittings that clearly haven't changed in decades are all bathed in a soft red glow from the ceiling lights. The wooden bar that lines nearly the whole length of the right-hand side of the space is clear of glasses when I arrive, with a set of idle pumps sitting in the middle. A faded square of orange paper with the words 'coconut rum punch on tap – $4.50' written in thick, black felt pen is stuck to one of the pumps. Fred is the only person in the club when I walk in. He is wearing a pair of blue Dickies trousers with a tucked-in t-shirt and a small, leather pork pie hat on his head. He locks the door behind me, then shuffles over to one of the high stools that line the bar and takes a seat.

'You know I got to practise soon,' he frowns, peering at me through his glasses in the soft red gloom.

'Oh I'd love to watch you if I can,' I gush.

Fred looks at me in surprise and then he frowns.

'I practise alone,' he says grouchily. 'I gotta practise and then after that I got to get the club ready for tonight 'cos we're doing a John Coltrane tribute night.'

The phone rings and Fred moves slowly down the length of the bar and behind it to where the receiver sits cradled in its bowl. As he goes to get the call I look to my left on the wall that's lined with a row of small, metal tables seating two-a-piece. Just right of the mounted cigarette machine that sits in the middle of the row of seats is a poster of Fred, marking a tour he did in Germany in 1979 for his Moers

Music release of *Another Day*. In the poster a handsome, muscular man poses in full-length profile, eyes closed, head turned down slightly, holding his glowing sax around his neck. He is dressed in a denim jacket and tight denim jeans, with thick, black sideburns sprouting from under a black, leather hat and reaching down almost to his chin. It's an image of Fred that's hard to equate with the man moving behind the bar.

Fred reaches the phone just as it stops ringing and kicks into ansaphone. His recorded voice asks the caller to leave a message and a brash-sounding woman 'with a party of people in from New York that night' asks, rudely, to be called back on a number. Fred shrugs, leaves the woman to bark into the soft, warm, empty silence of the club, and moves back round to the other side of the bar, where I'm sitting. He takes up his stool again.

For an hour or so we talk. He tells me about his life, his work as a musician in the city and his own recordings and slowly, as we speak, I can see that any outward harshness from this man was mere surface. It's a trait I'd begun to notice in Chicago people and a refreshing alternative to the plastic, surface quality of the 'have a nice day' crowd you find on the West Coast of America or the downright brashness of East Coasters. As Fred spoke, I warmed to the club.

The tribute night at the Velvet tonight, Fred tells me, is to honour John Coltrane whose birthday falls the following month on 29 September.

'There's no cover charge tonight because it's a special night,' says Fred. 'We want to do this for John Coltrane.'

I ask Fred why and as he tells me, his eyes light up. John Coltrane is one of his idols and he remains an absent mentor. He is soon lost in the past; talking about seeing Charlie Parker and John Coltrane play live and the influence they had on him as a young musician.

'They call Benny Goodman's music jazz music. But his music wasn't jazz music – it was dance music,' says Fred. 'It wasn't artistic. They called him the "King Of Swing" but really what he made was just dance music. He disbanded his bands a couple of times and he couldn't make it and at the end he started playing classical music again. Now

Duke Ellington kept playing and writing music until he died. Count Basie the same thing. John Coltrane the same thing. Charlie Parker the same thing. I don't think a lot of people understand that. They started calling Kenny G's music jazz – that's not jazz. That's not the music I was raised up with. Kenny G doesn't make jazz but he makes a whole bundle of money, and he can't even play as good as some of these kids that come down here.

'This music is an art. This is spontaneous improvisation and it's an art. I think Charlie Parker was an artist. John Coltrane was an artist. All of them were true artists and this music was their life. They didn't play down to people. They played what they felt. They played their life. They had no options. They didn't have a day job. All they had was music. Duke Ellington didn't have a day job but he kept a band going. I don't know how he did it but he did it. He kept all these people together all those years.

'That's what I was raised up on, just like the Europeans were raised up on classical music. That's the music that I, culturally, heard all of my life, from a young age. I remember seeing Charlie Parker in the 1940s. A lot of kids that came up after that didn't get a chance, if they were born in the 1950s or 1960s.

'I'm concerned about the history of the music. The origin of the music and where it came from. Who started the music and I look at it from an Afro-American perspective. Other people can have other different ideas about what's good music and good jazz but I've always looked at it from the traditional books and the music and the time that the music was created here and under the conditions. It's not African music – it's Afro-American music. It's got some European roots in it. The harmonies and stuff like that but the rhythm, that was basically the African influence brought over by the slaves who came to America – and this is what we deal with.'

During our chat Fred moves over to his saxophone case. As he picks up his case it's quite clear that I'm not leaving and despite his earlier protests, Fred makes no efforts to ask me to go. Apart from the soft red lighting that lines the main strip of the bar, the only other light burning in the place is a single spot on the ceiling in front of the stage.

From that single bulb a cool, white circle lights a space in the front of the stage and Fred stands under it as he unclips his case and takes out his horn.

'I don't play pop tunes, you know,' he says, peering up at me.

Fred starts blowing his horn, bent over slightly with one foot planted firmly in front of the other and I watch him. As he plays alone, in front of the stage, I recognise snatches of his tunes that I've heard on recordings. Snippets of the melody of his 'Ladies In Love' tune are woven into scale ascents and slick incidentals. He plays fast and then slow, eyes closed, as beads of sweat form on his brow and neck. The sweet harmonies of his sound combine with a strong rhythmic sensibility and as he blows, I think about what Fred had said earlier about the origins of jazz music.

According to Fred, jazz music in its earliest form was made up of a combination of African rhythm and European harmony and as Fred plays his horn, to an audience of one in his otherwise empty club, I realise that that's the point, that's it in a nutshell. Jazz music is where European-American culture and African-American culture became common in American culture all those years ago. Here in Chicago, suffering the same cultural and racial problems of any city in America, jazz music is still expanding and growing creatively. It's through jazz that artists like Fred choose to express themselves and, as they do, they keep up an important cultural tradition and continue forging the kind of indelible, timeless, culture-spanning bonds that only music can make.

Fred is pouring sweat as he practises but he doesn't stop to mop it up. In his space, under the single spot in the empty Velvet Lounge, it seems like he's oblivious to everything except the sounds he's making with his horn. He moves four- and two-bar phrases, playing a series of chord structures and feeding on different variations, but always bringing in a melody. Sometimes it's snatches of something I recognise and other times a melody phrase that seems familiar is quickly lost as Fred moves on. I recognise part of one tune as 'Our Theme', a composition that Fred recorded in 1996 with North Side tenor sax player Ken Vandermark's DKV trio on an Okka Disc album called

Fred Anderson & DKV Trio. If there's a shining example of the North and South Sides coming together to record, it's that album.

I'd seen Ken Vandermark play a gig with one of his many ensembles just a few nights previous to my visit to the Velvet Lounge. The venue was covert jazz den 3030, a converted church at 3030 West Cortland Street in the northwest of the city.

The 3030, it turned out, was run by Dave Rempis who also happened to be the alto and tenor sax player in Ken's Vandermark Five band. With no listings, signposts or other usual indications that this was a local venue of sorts, I was amazed that I actually found the place but once I got through the doors, up the wooden staircase and into the venue, I knew I'd done the right thing.

Chicago's current Mayor Daley – the 45th mayor of the city and the son of the Mayor Daley who reigned over the city in the mid-1950s – has made it very difficult for anyone in the city to obtain a liquor licence since he came into power in 1989. Pressure from Chicago church people – who believe alcohol to be the root of all evil – to cut down on the watering holes in the city has helped the current Mayor Daley's quest to dry out Chicago. The result has been that venues operating shy of the law have been springing up all over the city. These small hole-in-the-wall style rooms, where alcohol is sold from boxes under a counter, usually feature bands and musicians playing to a handful of people. The 3030 is one of these places. An elevated mixing desk sits where the pulpit once stood. At the back of the room, a double row of thin wooden benches, where churchgoers once sat, divides the space between the back of the room and the stage.

The Sound And Action trio is made up of Ken, Tim Daisy and Robert Barry. With these two drummers – Daisy playing faster and the seasoned drummer Barry, who used to play with Chicago's spaced-out, big band leader Sun Ra, playing slower – Ken plays his full complement of wind instruments. Shifting between tenor and baritone sax, clarinet and bass clarinet, the 90% improvised, 10% composition-based live show is a noisy, edge-of-the-seat experience and watching Ken and his band play that night at the 3030 opened up the exciting possibilities of this music. The unpredictability of the sound coming from that stage had the whole room lulled into an excited hush. Ken's band was setting the stakes the highest they could be that night, and that seemed to put the atmosphere in the room on a knife-edge.

After the gig I cornered Ken to ask him why he had opted to make up a band with himself and two drummers. On paper it seemed unlikely that the set-up would sound like anything more than a jam session, but it had worked.

'I was trying to find a way to work with Robert in a context that seemed to be really full of possibilities and the two-drummer thing worked really well because he really loves to play with drummers,' he told me. 'He was one of the first drummers to work with Sun Ra, when Ra was here in the Fifties. He talked about bands Ra would have with like five drummers in the band and how he liked doing that and that kind of keyed me into trying it with a trio. What's interesting about that group is to have Tim Daisy – he's about 26/27 years old and also a phenomenal musician – side by side with Robert. It's just great to see the whole way they approach the instrument.'

Ken, it turns out, moved to Chicago from Boston eight years ago to pursue music. Rather than play standards at weddings and cocktail parties, he found a job working in the museum shop at the city's Art Institute and spent his free time pursuing the music he loved. From knowing very few people in the city, he eventually got to play with people like Michael Zurang and even Chicago punk-rock band Jesus Lizard. Years of gigging and forging contacts eventually resulted in Ken kick-starting a North Side-based scene for improvised jazz music. In 1999 he was awarded a MacArthur prize for his work in the city. The MacArthur Fellows Program is a private, independent, grantmaking institution that awards 'unrestricted fellowships to talented individuals who have shown extraordinary originality and dedication in their creative pursuits and a marked capacity for self-direction'. Of his $250,000 in grant money, Ken ploughed half into putting on acts in the city, organising concerts, touring with bands and bringing European improvised jazz musicians to Chicago to play.

'The biggest thing that I want to obtain is a way to position improvised music in such a way that people hear it and see it as part of the entire music scene,' says Ken. 'One of the problems with improvised music is that people who aren't familiar with it think of it as being a specialist thing. People who play it are élitist and think you need to have 80,000 records and you need to know who Charlie Parker is, otherwise you can't understand what they're doing. I think there's lots of reasons for that, but the jazz media really perpetuates a very isolated, provincial view of the music. I find that incredibly frustrating.

'Through my own experience of touring and playing all over the world, it's clear to me that there's a whole audience who come from a rock background that is really ready to hear stuff that's played with a lot of passion, conviction and creativity. It's just that you need to get it to them somehow, you need to put it in a room that they're familiar with. I don't think the biggest problem is the music, I think the music is fine. I think the thing that makes it hard is making the music accessible where an audience is going to check it out. That's the advantage of playing at somewhere like the Empty Bottle even though it's essentially a rock club – it's totally expanded the audience that I play to. We basically have 100–120 people come to see us every Tuesday we play, which for any kind of music for any kind of band on a Tuesday every week to pull in that many people is pretty amazing. And obviously something in the music is communicating to those people. If I only played in places like the Green Mill or like a jazz gallery that whole audience wouldn't come because they're just not going to go to a jazz bar. The ideal thing is to do both. The biggest thing I'm trying to figure out is how to get the music thought of as having a viable place in everybody's life who's interested in music. You don't have to be a specialist, you don't have to study it and have a sense of its history before you can appreciate it.

'If a group like the Buena Vista Social Club can play in the US and be written about by a lot of people who know zero about Cuban music and have other people who know zero about Cuban music be excited about it then for me it's not too big a leap to get that same kind of excitement about Peter Brotzmann's large group, full of international people playing together. It's a large ensemble with some of the best musicians in the world, period. You just need to get people to see it that way. And I think a large part of that is trying to access the media and get them to rethink what music is about now. Because if you're still working with these categories you're going to really miss out on a lot of what's going on in music. So many musicians are working outside those boundary lines now because they're looking for vitality and energy.'

It's this excitement that Ken feels lies at the heart of what is going on in the improvised jazz scene in Chicago's North Side. At the 3030 his audience is made up of young, sharp-dressed city slick types, student trendies, jazz nuts with pointy beards and a smattering of older jazz heads. The atmosphere is exciting because the music is on the edge – and yet it's something the crowd can get into. But, says Ken, it's not just the improvised jazz scene that's causing a stir in the city.

'One of the things I really like about the music scene in general here in Chicago is that there's lots of different kinds of music happening,' says Ken. 'There are all sorts of musicians playing regularly in the city, playing all kinds of music and if we're not playing together we're really aware of other people's work. Generally speaking I find the musicians here are very supportive of each other and I think in part it's because the economics of living in the city aren't as severe as, let's say, a place like New York. It's really expensive to live in New York, even living in Brooklyn now is really expensive or Queens or whatever, so people can live here and have a job and play concerts and survive you know. Most of the musicians I play with have a day job of some kind and I'm fortunate now that I'm at the point where I can just work on the music and make ends meet. Most of the players here have day jobs but they are able to play and able to work in the music they want to and there's places to perform so it's not like 100 musicians trying to play in one club. There's a lot of different venues and to make a comparison to NY I'd say there are as many opportunities and places to play in Chicago for improvised music as in NY and there's probably about a quarter of the musicians.

'This city is in the middle of nowhere – so people in the Mid West who are creative, who want to get out of whatever cornfield they are in, are going to come here. There's a certain type of person in the creative pursuits who'll probably end up here. There are less economic restrictions here, so there's a higher chance that people will take chances on going to see a band play. A lot of the concerts I do are like $5 or less, whereas in other cities it'll cost $15 to go see someone you never heard of.'

Ken has no plans to leave Chicago. He describes working with Fred Anderson as a 'really big deal' and his approach to music is the same as Fred's: they both feel like they're still learning. Ken is in his 30s. Fred is twice his age. I think about that as I watch Fred play his sax in the Velvet Lounge, blowing into the silent warmth of the club that will soon be filled with the evening's crowd. Later that night, long after Fred has packed away his horn, the band has taken the stage and all the tables and bar stools are full, I think about something Fred had said earlier that evening. The Velvet Lounge, he'd told me, might have been under his charge for the past twenty years but it could be taken away from him at any minute.

'I'm just struggling here just trying to keep this place going,' Fred had said. 'I'm not making money. But this is my life. I don't have the money to have a big building. I don't own the building. I'm just renting it. Day by day and month by month, so I could be out of here any time. I don't get no overwhelming support. I don't get any money from the city. I don't get grants or anything. I'm just a regular business corporation and they treat me just like they treat any other kind of business and if I can't afford it I go out of business.'

Under Mayor Daley's new rules, Fred wouldn't be able to open another tavern like the Velvet Room without getting a licence to serve food and drink too. This, he says, would just be too much hassle. If the Velvet Lounge closed then another of Chicago's jazz institutions would go under just like all those places that closed down all those years ago. Despite efforts by the likes of AACM-affiliated trumpet player Malachi Thompson, whose Kenwood Community Organisation on 47th Street is striving to retain and restore some of the musical and cultural history of Chicago's South Side, it seems that the city's legacy as a jazz town is of little importance to authorities. Fred looks sad when I ask him about what the South Side's music scene used to be like.

'It used to be music on every street in this part of the South Side. 47th Street, 63rd Street, 43rd Street: all in the neighbourhoods there. Places like this and rooms where smaller bands played. Then all of a sudden the juke boxes came in and then after the juke boxes and DJs came in, that just killed all of the music. So we don't really have anything. On top of that the city changes the rules. That, I would imagine, killed all of the clubs. Killed all the venues. Now I'm pretty much the only one left. On the North Side it's maybe a little bit different, I don't know 'cos I'm not so much concerned about that. I'm concerned about what's going on here. I can't really say why they done it or how they done it but it seems to be working that way, against the South Side.

'Gerri's Palm Tavern on 47th Street, that's long gone too. She had been around when Dizzy Gillespie and that came to town. They all used to come to her tavern. They got rid of her. They tore the building down. She was probably one of the last ones around. I don't even really know how long I'm going to be here. They are really trying to wipe out all the places like this in Chicago.'

As Fred practised that night, with no one else around but me to see, I sensed in his playing the struggle that comes with being a truly creative musician. Improvised music provides everybody who plays it with the possibility of making something better and sometimes it's just nice to observe that struggle. When a musician's performance looks and sounds like it's seat-of-the-pants but in fact comes from a deep, innate understanding of what they are doing, you can get an eerie sense of their life through the music. That's when it gets really good. When it's not happening it's not happening at all and when things break down, it's interesting to see what someone does to get things back to a point where they work again. Musically that had always seemed more interesting to me than a really slick horn section or a pre-planned, well-rehearsed next move. Watching Fred Anderson practise his horn, sweating under the single spotlight in his small watering hole, I sensed the struggle of a man who's survived 74 years in a hard city, striving to live and play his music; always keeping things on his own terms.

4 Who's In Da House?

SOME DAYS the heat in the city is enough to make you want to surrender, cancel all appointments for the day and head down to the lake to find a shady spot near the water to while away those long hot hours. It was on those kinds of days that I felt very envious of Duke, sitting in the shade of the maple trees on his cool, green bench in front of the fountain. When the heat is way up in the hundreds and I am trussed up for a meeting or off to run an errand somewhere around the city, I would always cast an eye towards Duke, sitting as cool as a cucumber and staring at the pretty fountain. I always looked his way when I passed him on the other side of the street but he never saw me. Sometimes I'd walk right by him, on my way to the subway or over to the bank and my face would be ready to crack a smile if he looked my way but he never did. Since that day we'd spoken I'd only caught his eye once. I'd been rushing past to grab the last taxi, mumbling to myself about being late and I'd almost forgotten to look Duke's way. Then, just as I was about to get into the cab, I'd looked up and was sure our eyes had met through the hazy drizzle of the fountain. In his old eyes I saw what I was convinced was the first twinkle of a smile and so I grinned right back at him and jumped in the cab.

Like an ancient barometer it seemed Duke was always right about the weather, even though he'd often be sitting there on his bench well before the character of the day had set in for definite. I eventually learned that if you wanted to know what sort of day it was going to be, weather-wise, you'd be better off simply forgetting the TV and radio reports, which were so often wrong, and instead popping down to Duke's bench to check out what he was wearing that day.

It was on one of the hottest days I'd encountered in the city that I had to make a trip up to Bucktown to the camera shop by the subway station to buy a particular battery I needed. Even though it was just one stop on the El to Damen and I could have walked, I decided the icy cool of the air-conditioned train would be much better than a heat-beaten stroll up Division – so I'd ambled past Duke, down the subway and onto the train.

Bucktown, aside of Wicker Park, was one of the best places in the city to hang out as far as I was concerned. You could go shopping for clothes and records, eat lovely food, hang out in street-front bars and cafés all day and night, go to a club in the evening, catch a movie and do pretty much anything that makes city living so attractive. For what seemed a long time, the city still had that honeymoon thrill for me that any new place does. The thing I've always loved about any city, anywhere, is the way that ripples of change run through it, with the style and atmosphere of certain areas changing in time with the generational shifts of their inhabitants. A city takes these changes in its stride, welcoming new styles like a fashion-conscious *grand dame*. Weather can beat down a relentless assault, evolution might take its toll on landmarks, war may even rip through a city and threaten to raze it to the ground – but the city will always bounce back, lovingly nursed back to health by its faithful, tireless inhabitants. In cities, these millions of people strive to survive and work to keep themselves and their beloved homes going. Meanwhile, the metropolis itself burns away like an insatiable fire, consuming whatever you put into the hungry furnace that keeps it going then ripping out for more. It's this constant fuelling and input that continually renews the city's identity, as different areas get facelifts that in turn attract new hordes of city dwellers.

In any city, however, for as long you live there, you get a delicious sense of anonymity that you could never get in a provincial town or village. But it's the delightful absolute anonymity of the first few weeks in a new city that is most delectable. It was those exhilarating early days in Chicago, free of the demands of friends and family and stripped of the shackles of my previous life, that were for me the headiest of all. The sound, smell and look of the city were like the shivery thrills of a first kiss. Every corner I turned brought a new sensory input with it that left my head reeling and my heart light and through it all I was just a stranger, with nothing to go on and no one to go there with.

It was a bit of a surprise, then, in those first few weeks of being in this strange and wonderful city, to be walking through the mid-morning buzz of Bucktown and hear someone shout out my name. The yell was a very masculine holler and it came from a car whizzing past me. That very same car, with an unidentified driver at the wheel, then reversed and screeched to a halt, Starsky and Hutch style, right in front of me. Hearing my name shouted across the road was like being pulled up out of a deep dream. As I came to in the bright heat, my head was spinning trying to work out who the hell could be calling out to me in this foreign place. Then it clicked. I was in Bucktown and in the whole of the city there was only one person who knew me well enough to recognise me walking down the street in their neighbourhood. It had to be the DJ/producer Derrick Carter.

After meeting Fred Anderson and spending a cosy afternoon and evening listening to his story, I'd thought about his statement: 'then the juke boxes and DJs came in, and that just killed all of the music'. It had been a fair comment on Fred's part, but in life, as in music, one door rarely closes without another one throwing itself wide open. DJ culture, in Fred's eyes, might not even register as an important part of the city's musical history but it was out of that culture that a whole new strain of music emerged. House music – the precursor to the electronic dance music culture that is a global phenomenon today – was born here in Chicago. It's a style of music that was initially directly linked to dancing in nightclubs. Now, though, it has become a form that incorporates hundreds of different strands of sound, both live and electronic, and that is enjoyed in and out of discos right across the world. It's the term 'dance music' that pulls all those strands together and it was dance music that emerged as the biggest musical revolution at the end of the 20th century. It's still going strong today and Derrick Carter, who had just opened the door of his car, leaned out and beckoned me to hop inside its cool, black, leather interior, is one of its main purveyors.

Derrick's story is a typical Chicago music man's tale. He's worked hard to get where he is. He's faced adversity and setbacks to make his name but he's done it anyway and, like many Chicago musicians of note, it's through live performance that he's earned his dues. To people like Fred Anderson, DJing might not be a relevant art form but if Fred looked closely at the art of DJing and DJ culture he would see that the bones of it aren't so different from the improvised music that he plays. A DJ is playing someone else's records for sure, but in piecing together those records – whether they're instrumental tracks, songs or a capellas – what the DJ is doing is creating new music. There's a lot of practice involved too. Sure: it's not that difficult to mix two records together using two turntables and a mixer – but there is an art in knowing which record will fit exactly with the next in mood, theme, style and key. The difference between a good DJ and a bad DJ is about the same as the difference between a good musician and a bad musician. If you haven't put the practice in, then it's fairly obvious once you take to the decks. Good DJs play in the moment, picking up the mood and atmosphere of what is going on in a room and, in their heads, composing the perfect soundtrack to that mood. Mixing two records of the same tempo together is child's play. A good DJ goes beyond that, though, taking records that might not be so obviously matched to the average listener and weaving them together in a blend that hits right to the heart of people listening. But DJing isn't just about mixing records together. It's also about the fresh sounds that are made using the instrument and the tools. The instrument is the decks and the tools are the records. Turntablism – the art of picking out breaks in records and scratching them into new rhythms that make entirely new, live-based pieces – came directly out of the New York hip hop scene that emerged in the early Eighties. Turntablism is just another strand of DJ culture that's as globally popular as other forms of dance music. But it was here in Chicago that house music actually emerged, directly out of the ashes of the black, gay, post-disco club scene.

Derrick is in a hurry to get back to his home-based studio and put the finishing touches to a record he's working on. In the car behind him are two other local DJ/producers who make up part of his gang. Tim Schumaker and JT Donaldson wait patiently as Derrick and I make plans to hook up later. I ask him to drop me at the nearest bus stop that's headed back towards downtown.

I STEP OUT of the cool, air-conditioned bus onto the baked pavement of South Jefferson Street and the heat hits me like a hot, damp blanket. The air is like steam, vapourising as it hits my skin into beads of sweat that prickle my forehead. I look down at a shiny quarter pressed into the freshly laid tarmac at the side of the road. A steady flow of traffic cuts through the afternoon buzz on this trendy, West Side industrial-zone street and in tune with the heated growl of the traffic is the sound of human activity getting into the swing of the day. Across the busy throughway in the near distance is the Greyhound bus depot where rows of sleek coaches bask idly, like silver lozenges sparkling in the midday sun. The sky above them shivers against their heat as people, like tiny insects, file out of the terminus. I stand still and watch them scatter, squinting in the blinding sun, and then take another look directly in front of me at the nondescript warehouse building hunched directly across the street.

This building looks just like any other on this strip of road: a squat, silent block, low-piled against the sky. Like the buildings surrounding it, this one might have been recently refurbished. Except for the freshly painted front door and the sight of plants and furniture through the big rectangular windows, the rest of the building is drab and dusty, its dull brickwork outshone by the dazzling silvers and icy glass of Chicago's impressive skyline marching into the wide blue sky. But this particular building – the sign outside reads 206 – is so much more than it appears from the outside. If foundations hold histories and walls keep long-lost secrets, then this building, like any other, has stories to tell. Whatever went on in there in the late Seventies and early Eighties clearly isn't going on any more but the fact remains that the heartbeat of Chicago's house music history pumped its first rudimentary beats here, in the basement of this silent, unassuming building in this up and coming part of town.

It's hard to imagine then that it was here, at the tail end of the 1970s, that a 21-year-old, New York-based DJ called Frankie Knuckles took up a gig that would initiate a whole new style of music. Knuckles was a disco DJ who, alongside his cohort Larry Levan, played in gay discos in the pre-Aids heady days that were defined in New York clubs by promiscuity, drug-taking, dancing and fun-fuelled party music. It was after his residency at the NYC boys' hang-out The Continental Baths that Knuckles heard about the job going in Chicago at a new club called the Warehouse. The job was initially offered to Levan who turned it down in favour of a post at NYC club The Paradise Garage. Knuckles took it and his fate was sealed. He brought his style of New York DJing to Chicago at a time when the club scene in the city was nothing to speak of. There were DJs, for sure, but those that played would simply take their boxes of funk and blues tapes and 7-inch discs down to a local tavern to play music while people drank.

Knuckles' arrival in the city in March 1977 changed all that. He took up his residency at the 600-capacity Warehouse, the same building I'm standing outside now, as soon as he arrived in the city. Word of the parties soon spread and for one day a week, running from Saturday night through to Sunday afternoon, Knuckles would play disco and soul music to a crowd of largely black, gay party people. Back then, this near West Side neighbourhood, now known as West Town, was a deserted industrial zone but, despite the club's desolate location, the reputation of the parties grew around the city. As Chicago's only black, gay disco – with Knuckles as the city's most prominent black, gay DJ – the weekly parties very quickly became oversubscribed. His weekly parties would attract around 2,000 revellers. Crammed into three floors, these parties were hot, sweaty, sexy events that the crowd of regulars would build up to each week. Often, they would sleep all day before the event in order to have the staying power required to make it through until Sunday afternoon.

By the time Knuckles had arrived in Chicago, the disco revolution in New York was shifting from the solely gay, underground clubs in the city to the more homogenised, fashion and celeb-infused venues like Studio 54. But that was New York. As a blue-collar city, the hard-working ethic of Chicago bred a different kind of disco scene that was centred around the Warehouse and left to thrive in an undiluted, heady concoction of energetic music, loyal followers and regular parties. This mutant disco scene remained underground – it was a black and gay scene that pumped away unnoticed by others – and with it came the hype and notoriety that turned on legions of party and music lovers to the sounds that were coming out of the Warehouse. Knuckles' early sets were very reminiscent of the sounds he'd played back in New York – early Salsoul Records, songs by Gamble & Huff, soul and funk tunes.

The energy of the parties required that Knuckles DJed in a continuous mix and in order to keep the atmosphere going, he began to tailor his sets for this purpose. At home, before he was due to play, he would re-edit the tunes in his crate using a reel-to-reel tape recorder. Choosing parts of a particular record that he knew had an extra incendiary effect on the dancefloor, Knuckles would cut and paste and segue together elongated versions of certain songs that he would road-test in the club at the weekends. This was at a time when single records in full, extended, 12" format were very rare – the first 'extended dance mix' was actually an elongated version of The Tramps' 'That's Where The Happy People Go', out on Atlantic Records in 1975. To make up for the lack of extended 12s, Knuckles had to get creative and would cobble together his own mixes. He began deconstructing original tunes so that they worked in this alternative club environment and injected extra energy and vitality into the party. Some of the songs he altered would turn into a finished version that focused on the repetition of a particular vocal or a certain part of a song. These reel-to-reel re-edits might have been rude, cobbled together, purely functional DJ tools – but sewn between the grooves of those early efforts were the first seams of the global DJ and dance music culture. Knuckles would enhance these elongated disco tracks by adding beats from a cheap drum machine that he'd hook up to the system in the club, providing an underpinning pulse that would fuel dancers for hours on end.

I cross the street until I'm standing right outside 206 and imagine the line of people streaming in on a Saturday night. The three-floor building that housed the club had an entrance that, back then, took you straight to the top floor where chairs and sofas were scattered to create a seating area. Another staircase led to the basement where you could get juices and other refreshments but it was towards the middle floor, where the dancefloor was, that most people made a beeline when they entered the club. By the end of the 1970s disco music was more about John Travolta and *Saturday Night Fever* than it was about edgy, exciting, new music and getting down on the dancefloor. Here at the Warehouse, though, disco had mutated and was already paving the way for something new.

The term 'house music', as dance music lore has it, came directly from the Warehouse. People who attended those weekly events would troop down to local record stores like Imports Etc and ask for 'the kind of music you'd hear at the Warehouse'. Some say 'house' started out as a section in the record stores where the kind of records you'd hear at the Warehouse were lumped together to be sold. Others say that 'house' just referred to the kind of music Knuckles would play at the club. Many DJs say that house music just referred to this new brand of party music, including anything and everything that fitted the mood, played at a tempo and blended in a manner that would make you want to dance. Many DJs scoff at the term, dismissing it as just another effort to classify music – but the term exists, has a history and was born in Chicago. It has since spread all over the world, becoming synonymous with youth culture across continents.

Frankie Knuckles still works as a DJ and producer today. Although he tends to shrug off the title, he has been called the 'Godfather of house' in the US and abroad. Knuckles lived and worked in Chicago for many years. He left the Warehouse in 1983 to open his own venue, a new club called the Power Plant. By then, another local DJ called Ron Hardy was hosting weekly parties at a club called the Music Box, controlled by the people who'd owned The Warehouse. The Music Box parties attracted a more sexually and ethnically mixed crowd than Knuckles' bashes but the soundtrack was largely the same. Hardy would play a continuous mix of disco, funk, soul and reggae records and pepper the blend with reel-to-reel, extended re-edits of songs. While Knuckles would focus on songs when he Djed, it was Hardy who really worked the idea of looping parts of instrumental tracks. Hardy would take instrumentals and loop them to make monotonous yet hypnotic-sounding groove tracks and then play these under other song-based records, underlaying the grooves with drum machine beats. The sound system in the Music Box was renowned for being loud but with these trance-inducing tracks added to the potion, the overall effect was amazing. It wasn't long before kids who came to hear Hardy DJing at the Music Box became inspired by what they heard and started to try and create their own versions of Hardy's live, cobbled-together tracks.

One such local was a young postman named Marshall Jefferson. He remembers getting turned on to the club scene in the city for the first time.

'There was this girl at the post office named Lynne Montgomery and she used to dress a lot crazier than a lot of the other women at the post office,' says Marshall. 'Finally I said to her, why do you dress like that, where do you go? It turned out she went to the Warehouse and the Music Box. I didn't know anything about that. I was just interested 'cos she had curves. So she took me to the Music Box, Ron Hardy was the DJ that night, and I got into the music. It was the loudest music I had ever heard in my life before or since. I'd never heard music that loud. I felt it in my chest that night. The kick drums were moving me, they were "boom, boom, boom". I don't mean emotionally moving me, I mean physically. I was into it. I was there, man. That's when I started going there for the music. I was still going to the Copper Box, Club 69, Godfathers, Memphis, y'know to "pull", but I was spending more and more time at the Music Box. And then they were telling me about Frankie Knuckles and the Power Plant so I went there too. In the end I gave up all the pulling joints. I just got all the way into the music.

'I had already started DJing when Jesse Saunders made his first record, "On and On". Some time after that, a friend of mine, who played guitar, took me to a guitar centre in Chicago. The sales guy was telling me about this sequencer where a normal person can play keyboards like a real keyboard player and my friend was saying "ah, that's bullshit, I take lessons, you gotta go to school, you gotta learn it" but I said "I believe I'm gonna buy it". I felt inspired because I knew Jesse Saunders played all his own instruments on his record. By then I was DJing and he was a DJ like me. So I bought it. The guy was telling me "hey, you don't want this sequencer and not have a keyboard to play, do you?", so I bought the keyboard. Then he said "you don't want to have this sequencer and this keyboard and not have a drum machine, do you?", so I bought the drum machine.'

Jesse Saunders' 'On And On', a stripped-down version of the old Salsoul classic, came out in 1983 and became one of the first official 'house' records. A year after Saunders released 'On And On', local businessman Larry Sherman started up the Trax label to cater for the pool of young, local producers who were churning out house tracks. Saunders' next single 'Wanna Dance' was the first release on Trax that same year. Soon, all over the city, kids were going into their bedrooms using keyboards, drum machines and basic recording equipment and making house tracks. Marshall Jefferson was one of them.

'When you work at the Post Office in America, that's assumed by every establishment in America as a lifelong job, so they gave me credit on the spot so that's how I bought all this shit,' says Marshall. 'I bought nine grand worth of it. I bought a keyboard, a drum machine, a TB303, a 308, a 909, a 707, a mixer, everything. All my friends came round and said what a "stupid mother fucker" I was, buying all this stuff and not knowing how to play any of it. But after my friends left, I sat up with that equipment for two days and learned how to use it. At the end of those two days I wrote my first song. I made music! The next year I did "Move Your Body". The day I did it in the studio, I took it to Ron Hardy at the Music Box and he was listening to it in the headphones – it was on a cassette tape – and he immediately threw it over the system then played it six times in a row. The crowd flipped.'

Marshall's 'Move Your Body' was one of the follow-up club hits to come out of those early days of house. The record, released on Trax in

1986, became popular overseas and Marshall became popular with it, travelling abroad to Europe to do live versions of the song. But Marshall wasn't the only one inspired by what was going on in the clubs in Chicago. Other local kids who were wowed by what they'd heard down at the Warehouse and then the Power Plant and the Music Box were also sweating away at home trying to create their own versions of these early house music tracks. Jesse Saunders' 'On And On' was a simple if catchy track that opened the floodgates for others.

Slowly more producers started coming through; people like Larry Heard, DJ Pierre, Lil' Louis and Chez Damier. Chicago DJing star Farley Jackmaster Funk released a house version of Isaac Hayes' 'Love Can't Turn Around' in 1986 and it became the first dance record to break into the British Top Ten later that year.

A song by local producer DJ Pierre, called 'Acid Tracks', which was released under the name Phuture in 1986, featured acidy-style, squelchy noises achieved using a Roland TB-303 bassline machine and sparked the so-called 'acid house' scene. The 'acid house' hype created knee-jerk, panic headlines in the UK in the late Eighties because of its drug connotations. Here in Chicago, though, the scene was more about creativity than chemical abuse.

It wasn't just in the record shops and the clubs in Chicago that this scene flourished. The '21s and over rule' at the nightclubs would have excluded the younger generation of kids in the city from a big part of the flourishing house scene were it not for the radio. Local station WBMX played host to house music on a daily basis and employed five local DJs called The Hot Mix Five. The original five – Farley 'Jackmaster' Funk, Ralphi Rosario, Mickey 'Mixin' Oliver, Scott 'Smokin' Silz and Kenny 'Jammin' Jason – would play house mixes every day. It was these radio mixes that fuelled the younger generation of house fans to go out and buy records and try to emulate their 'hot mix' heroes.

During the mid-Eighties, house music was the sound of youth culture in the city. In 1987 Frankie Knuckles released the double a-side 'Baby Wants To Ride/I Need Your Love' through Trax and it became the next house release to achieve 'hit' status in Europe. But by that time, 'house' wasn't just about the music; instead, it was a term that applied to a whole movement that was sweeping Chicago. With it came a certain look – the 'house' style – and a dance called 'jacking' that was the 'house' dance. Jacking itself was as twitchy and frantic as the name suggests, but the sexual connotations of the word also applied. By the mid-Eighties, house was making itself heard outside of both Chicago and the US, while in the city kids were simply living, breathing and loving the music and the scene that had exploded around it.

Then, just as things were reaching fever pitch in the city, WBMX closed down. Frankie Knuckles left town and moved back to New York. The Warehouse was closed and the Music Box was on its last legs. Those first flushes of the exciting house music revolution were already transmuting and without the radio airplay that helped fuel record sales and keep the city's younger house fans going, the house scene headed back underground. It was this underground scene, and the house sounds that started to emerge from the South Side and Cabrini Green area of the city around that time, that Chicago house DJ and producer Curtis Jones (or Cajmere) found especially exciting.

THE SECOND wave of house in Chicago recruited new members, although the sound remained an urban phenomenon. If you drove around neighbourhoods like Cabrini Green in the very early Nineties, you would hear crazy minimal tracks, made on rudimentary home equipment, bleeping and squeaking out of the tower blocks. Alongside the similar-themed Radikal Fear label, Jones' Cajual and Relief Records labels dedicated their early releases to this kind of house sound. Jones, a college drop-out then still living on the South Side of the city, started the labels in 1990 and initially, due to lack of funds, ran them out of his grandmother's front room in her house on 77th Street and Wood. It's that same address that is printed on the paper disc and sleeves of the first Cajual release. In 1993 Jones got his own offices just minutes away from the Greyhound bus depot and the old Warehouse club.

Standing on the pavement outside the old Warehouse in the crippling afternoon heat, I decide to go and ring the doorbell of Jones' office to see if he's up for talking. When I get there, I find I'm lucky, because today is the one day of the week that he's in his office. Past-released Cajual and Relief records are hung on the wall in the brick, converted warehouse building and Jones is in a talkative mood.

'I liked a lot of the trackier stuff,' remembers Jones. 'The people I picked up in the beginning were people like Boo Williams, Glenn Underground, some Paul Johnson stuff, Ron Trent. I just really loved the music and I just loved – especially at that time – the feeling that it gave me and I wanted to keep it available for other people who appreciated it as I did. There was a time in the city when a lot of heads started going off to the hip hop/rap stuff and so the dance scene was like nothing going on. After hip house there wasn't anything new going on with house and that's when I was doing my stuff.'

Curtis remembers his burning desire to go out and dance that took him to the nightclubs in the city. Back then he wasn't particularly aware of the DJs themselves: it was just the music, the atmosphere and the chance to dance that was the impetus behind him going out.

'The thing I remember the most was that the parties were really fun,' he says. 'There was a lot of energy during the peak of house in the mid-Eighties. I don't even remember the names of the clubs. I think one was called CODs – that was a Lil' Louis club. There was Ron Hardy – he played at a place called Coconuts or something like that. Then there were clubs on Michigan; I forget the names. People I know were into that but I wasn't really into all that stuff. I wasn't into DJs, I just liked the music. I used to dance all the time. For me it was more about just going to hear good music. I was more into the artists and stuff than this club or that DJ. I must have gone to all the clubs though.

'What I remember the most was that there was a lot of energy at the parties and a lot of people, a lot of dancing and the music was diverse. Like they would play disco, they'd play tracks, they'd play industrial or new wave stuff. They played a lot of different stuff. There was a club called Medusas that played a lot of industrial music and I used to go there. That's where I'd get my industrial fix. But then a lot of stuff would cross over to the house stuff. The house DJs would be playing some of that stuff. They'd play Ministry. I don't know what

Liaison Dangereux was considered but they'd play that to death. Everybody played that. Everybody. Punk, industrial, house, everybody played that stuff. I think it was sort of considered more punky at that time. That was the crazier stuff.

'When I drive down that street where all the clubs were, I flashback a lot to when I was younger. I just danced a lot. I had a lot of energy. It was all about energy. When I think about it now what I see is a street full of traffic. I remember trying to find a parking space, then I remember getting into the club and just seeing how people would just snap when they heard some of the records. They would totally just lose their shit. That was when jacking was around. That's what I think about a lot. Jacking. I don't jack that much any more.

'Looking at it on an energy level, you're actually trying to get to a place where you feel like you're not so bound by your body and you're just at one with whatever you're interacting with. It could be a wall, a person, whatever. The music, in a way, possesses you to move and you're just feeling it and moving on a deeper or spiritual level. That's the way I see it. So jacking is a spiritual form of dance. But you look at a lot of tribal dancing and stuff and you could call that jacking 'cos it looks like that too. So to an observer it just probably looked like tribal dancing.'

The sparse rhythms, snappy beats and tougher-sounding bass lines of the Cajual, Relief and Radikal Fear releases marked a shift away from the often vocal-based early house sound. In the space of a decade, house music had gone from a feeling and a way of living that was experienced solely on the dancefloor to something that referred to a particular form. Making house music was a DIY process, with tracks crafted at home by young producers using whatever equipment they could get their hands on. House records were generally made using a 4/4 beat pattern, a bassline, a basic melody, vocals, samples and other manipulated sounds. It's a format that still defines house music today but it's in defining the sound, as far as Jones is concerned, that the original spirit of house has been somewhat lost.

'The scene is watered down because it's not as cohesive as it was,' says Jones. 'There are so many different subgroups in the group. Before it was house. That was it. But now there's house, deep house, progressive, trance, techno, so it's all over the place now. There were a lot more vocals and vocals with energy in the past, but now it's totally different.'

Later that day, when I hook up with Derrick at the Northside Tavern & Grill in Bucktown, I discover that he actually worked for Jones at Cajual Records for a couple of years, just at the time the label moved to the present offices.

'I was Prime Minister of hype there,' he grins. Shortly after that, Derrick started up his own Blue Cucaracha record label, through which he released his own productions.

Born in the Compton district of Los Angeles before moving to the suburbs of Chicago while barely out of nappies, Derrick hit his teenage years just as house music was emerging in the city. He remembers listening to the radio and hustling tapes of Ron Hardy DJing at the Music Box from older kids in the city and trying to mimic what he heard at home on his record deck and tape machine. He spent his youth 'shovelling a lot of snow' and saving up his lunch money to find the cash he needed to buy records. By the time he was 13, he could mix records proficiently and was the elected DJ at his pals' birthday parties. From there on, he built on his craft, going from the decks into the studio and back again.

Wind forward to today and through his current Classic Records Label, he provides an umbrella for a pool of local producers and DJs who release their music through him. Classic Records is co-run by Derrick and his UK-based partner Luke Solomon. Each Classic release shifts at least 4,000 units. Shifting that amount of vinyl on every release would probably keep the label just bubbling along. But Classic Records is actually a success story in terms of independent, transatlantic labels. The 2001-released 'Bushes' track by German producer Markkus Nikkolai got licensed to a major UK label for a healthy six-figure sum, after having success in the clubs and on the radio. Today, the label continues to be one of the best house music independent labels in the world and much of the talent pool drawn on for Classic comes from right here in Chicago. Everything that comes out on the label is selected and overseen by Derrick and Luke and, in 2002, Derrick put out his debut solo production album through Classic. The record *Squaredancing In A Round House* was an opus that drew on all Derrick's past influences, including the early house sound that came out of the city, Latino music, jazz, funk and soul. Derrick sings on the album and most of the tracks feature full songs or lyric snippets written by Derrick himself. It's a theme he's going to expand on for the next long-player that he's already working on every day in his home studio.

'I work on music during the week,' says Derrick. 'That's my day job. That's what I do every day. For most parts I'm in the studio trying to pull inspiration out of my ass. Out of the ether. At the moment I'm interested in sonic texture. I'm looking to kind of make sounds like they have a texture. Little sprockets or cogs on it or this sound sounds like it's furry. I did this one track and the bass sound, to me, sounded slobbery like a slobbery dog. Just drooling. I use that as a good reference point for me to do these things that have this texture. If I'm not in the studio working then I'm DJing abroad. When I'm at home I try to cut my DJing down just to be able to spend time at home or hanging out around the city.'

Chicago writer Nelson Algren's *The Neon Wilderness*, a book of short stories about the city, had stoked my desire to visit Chicago. He wrote the book in 1947 and his plain-speaking yet poetic and harshly honest depiction of Chicago was what made me realise that city life was the only life for me. Algren once famously said that 'loving Chicago is like loving a woman with a broken nose'. The way Derrick describes his city to me makes me think of that.

'Chicago is like three different cities rolled into one. She's a strange city for sure,' says Derrick. 'The South Side of Chicago is definitely a different thing to anything else but that's because it has this sort of mystique like "don't go to the South Side, they'll fuck you up on the South Side". It's not really like that down there and even in the worst places good things are going on. Out of poverty and oppression come beautiful things sometimes. Like the idea of a rose growing from the hard ground. It's kind of cool.

'South Side, West Side and North Side are very different in terms of, like, migratory patterns and the people that settled them. There's different attitudes and fashions to each area too. What you can get away with and what you can't change as you move around the city. You can see it in the girls that come from different parts of the city. On the West Side you get some really crazy hair. You see West Side girls they have hair with like ten colours going on and gold all over everything. South Side girls are more like booty girls. They wear tight pants and shirts and are real easygoing. North Side girls are prissy, a little bit more uptight.

'I like Chicago women. Like all the girls I know here. This is a generalisation but all the women I encounter are like really strong women. They like roll up their sleeves and say: "move, I'll get it" and are just like: "I can do it too". I dig that – like not trying to go: "ah, I can't, I'm a woman". Chicago women are like: "let me get in there". They curse like sailors. They can kick your ass a little bit if they have to. Put up or shut up. I like that a lot about the city because Chicago has a real "just do it, shut up" kind of attitude. It's cool. Don't sweat it.'

As a teenager growing up in the city, it was DJ culture that spoke to Derrick. He got two scholarships to go to Illinois University and started his first year but couldn't pick a major. Eventually he realised he wasn't that interested and dropped out. From college, he started working in local record store Imports Etc and from there he worked at Gramaphone Records, near to where we are sitting now. Derrick got into the music when he was a teenager. Clubs like the Music Box and the Power Plant were having their heyday but he was too young to get into them. Instead he would listen to the radio and do his own parties for kids in his neighbourhood. By the time Derrick was old enough to get into clubs, he'd already made a name for himself as a DJ in the city. A new wave of nightclubs had opened in the city but now, says Derrick, house music is all over Chicago.

'There's probably ten places up and down Division where you can go and hear house. They're not clubs. They're like bar/club kind of places – smaller and a bit more intimate. Then there's clubs like Slick's, Zentra, Red Dog. You can dance to house music every night of the week now.'

Frankie Knuckles moved back to Chicago again in the mid-Nineties. Bending in conspiratorially and whispering over the last remaining crumbs of his sandwich, Derrick tells me that after nearly a twenty-year hiatus, Frankie is about to do another party in the city. The weekly, Sunday afternoon tea–dance-style bash is starting in the city soon, hosted by Frankie and featuring him playing all night. The new club Hydrate is in 'boys' town', says Derrick, referring to the East Lakeview neighbourhood around 2800 Halsted. I ask Derrick if he thinks that Frankie doing his own gig in the city again is that important to Chicago-based house fans and his eyes widen as he breathes in sharply and places a hand to his chest.

'He's the godfather,' he replies.

I EVENTUALLY get to speak to Frankie himself, just weeks after he has started his new weekly event at Hydrate and ask him how he feels about being called the 'Godfather Of House'.

'I don't think about it,' shrugs Frankie.

Frankie has been playing the same kind of music for years. It's the music he started out playing back in the early days of the Warehouse. The only difference about what he plays now is that the equipment he uses and the records he plays on that equipment have evolved to create a slicker-sounding set.

'I'm playing like I've always played,' Frankie says. 'I play one song after another after another and you're talking about a six- or an eight-hour set with song after song after song. I like energetic music that's laced with voices, harmonics and melodies. I don't play that many instrumentals.'

These days Frankie lives in the West Loop neighbourhood that he lived in when he first moved to Chicago back in 1977 and his place now is just minutes from the spot where the Warehouse was held every Saturday night. When Frankie first moved to Chicago he lived in the club, looking after his pet project 24 hours a day, bedding down on a cot that was stashed behind the decks in the club. In those days he remembers this part of the West Loop as pretty deserted, with not even a grocery store within walking distance. Now, the West Loop area, just minutes away from the Warehouse, the Greyhound bus depot and Union Station, is one of the most sought-after places to live and hang out in Chicago. Frankie's house is just opposite Oprah Winfrey's Harpo studios. On nearby Randolph Street, which used to be home to the city's farmers' market, is the trendy 'restaurants row' where all the best eateries in the city are wedged into a line. According to Frankie, it's down to Oprah opening her studio here 15 years ago that all this 'splendour' came to the neighbourhood. Now developers have bought up most of the old warehouses and turned them into luxury apartments. In the time it's taken house music to come out of the city and spread its rhythmic beats across the world, the very spot that it emerged from – a desolate, unused part of the city – has metamorphosed and is flourishing as one of the hottest spots in Chicago.

5 True Blues

WAKING UP in a strange bed, in a strange city, can sometimes be disorientating. Usually it happens during the first few days: you wake with a start and for a few frantic moments don't remember where you are or what is real. In those few bleary instants, as you struggle to identify your surroundings and flick through the files of your recent memory, life is on hold, hanging in mid-air in tiny technicolor pieces. As you wait the agonising moments it takes for these bits to fall into place you are, for no more than a second, in no man's land. Lost in your head, somewhere in the world.

That happened to me a few times during my first few weeks in Chicago. Usually it was the slices of bright sunlight piercing the soft, cool gloom of my cosy room through the horizontal wooden blinds that brought me round, cutting through my confusion and pulling me to consciousness. When this happened I would lie in my bed, watching the thousands of specks of dust swirling in the shining spears. In those moments, hazy from a night's sleep, it was hard to escape the fact that those specks, surging and twisting in the new day's sun, were all that life amounted to in the end. It was a comforting feeling. Like thousands before and after me, I was just waking up to another day in the city.

The day, it turned out, was a Tuesday. I'd always liked Tuesdays. After Monday's fierce blow it was Tuesday that welcomed the week in properly; a day full of promise and possibility. It wasn't long before I was positioned by the stop for the number 70 bus heading east on Division towards the lake.

Mid-morning, mid-week, mid-town; and still the hot, yellow sand that kissed the shore of Lake Michigan by the edge of Lake Shore Drive, just near the Magnificent Mile shopping district on North Michigan Avenue, was scattered with sunbathers. Michigan Avenue begins at this spot. Looking towards it, I paused before ducking into the subway under the busy main road to get to the beach and I saw the hordes of shoppers around me heading towards the dazzling stretch that was home to Gucci, Prada and Max Mara, among others. During the winter holiday season this area around the top of North Michigan Avenue is turned over to the Magnificent Mile Lights Festival, when the streets and buildings are lit up with sparkling lights and the busy road is turned over to street sales and live music. For the rest of the year, it's just a shopper's dream, a fairytale funland for those who lust after designer labels and love to dally in department stores. To me, that seemed more like torture on a day like today.

While I was heading for the beach, all around me were well-heeled women and men of all ages. It was the women that astounded me: alone and in pairs, faces caked with perfectly applied make-up in spite of the heat and shielded from the morning glare of the sun by large, dark and obviously expensive designer shades. These painted dolls, trussed up and fierce, were headed towards the glittering emporiums in droves. From where I was standing, the pavement stretch on both sides of Michigan Avenue was packed to the edges, as hundreds of shoppers, office workers, tourists and dawdlers buzzed like worker bees in the hot air.

After gazing upon this soup for a moment, it was a relief to duck down into the cool, concrete underpass and stroll free under it all; the hum of traffic and the beep of car horns above me seemed suddenly miles away. By the time I emerged again into the hot sunlight, I was on the promenade, just steps away from the powdery sand and only a few yards from the cool, cyan spread of the lake.

Although surrounded by sandy beaches, Lake Michigan is still a lake and during the summer months news reports on TV, radio and in the papers assess the fecal count of the water to let you know when it's safe to swim.

The Tuesday I went there, it turned out, was a 'safe' day to swim. But even on days when news reports warned to stay out of the water, I would see people frolicking in the shallow parts when I went past the lake. Lake Michigan is the third largest of the Great Lakes and the only one that's totally within the United States, with a basin that drains parts of Wisconsin, Illinois, Indiana and Michigan. The lake discharges into Lake Huron in the northeast and through the Straits of Mackinac at a rate that allows for a total change of water every hundred years. It also sits as a link in the waterway system that reaches out east to the Atlantic Ocean and south along the Mississippi down to the Gulf of Mexico. The coastline stretches for nearly two thousand miles and cuts through four states, but only 27 of those miles belong to Chicago. Deserted sand dunes border the eastern and southern shores of the lake and the northern region is thick with forests. Right by the beginning of Chicago's sparkling shopping district, however, the lake shore is a city beach teeming with human life.

I lay in a patch of shade by the lifeguard's wooden look-out post, with the warm sand cushioning my legs and stomach. I had a perfect view of the rest of the beach, the promenade and the city behind it that afternoon. The heart of downtown Chicago was just a short jog away. But today, as I relaxed on the sand and looked at the fabulous city skyline, downtown felt remote and far away.

To the left of the picture and set against a cloudless sky, I could see the Sears Tower looming above the other gleaming skyscrapers. Until 1996, this was the tallest structure in the world, rising high at 1,450 feet. Then the Petronas Towers, in Kuala Lumpur took the title of the world's tallest building. 'The building in Kuala Lumpur is only the world's tallest because of an aerial at the top,' one outraged city-proud person had told me on the plane on my way over to Chicago. If you are 'into views', this same person had said, the sight of Chicago from the top of the Sears Tower, where you can get a coffee or a cocktail to accompany the view, is the best in the city.

The world's first skyscraper was actually built in Chicago, as it happens, in the Loop's central business district. Today the Monadnock

Building, the tallest load-bearing masonry structure in the world, still sits calmly in this part of town, while newer, more glittery edifices have sprung up around it.

Sitting in the sand and leaning against the warm wooden shaft of the lifeguard's look-out that afternoon, I could see joggers, skaters, cyclists and strollers crossing the wide promenade. They were tiny specks against the staccato skyline and they moved faster than the jam-blocked traffic behind them. Their lithe bodies and healthy skins contrasted sharply with the glow of their tight-fitted, fluoro-coloured shorts and vests. They were like a salute to summer. In front of them, in the sand, groups of friends and families were sitting next to couples and solo sun-worshippers – all basking in the midday heat.

My eyes hidden with big, dark sunglasses, I pretended to read my copy of the *Reader*, Chicago's free weekly paper, while surreptitiously watching the pair directly in front of me. With my head resting on my arms I could see the two men, a definite couple, lying outstretched in the sun's rays. With their feet just a metre away from me, I could hear them bickering about suntan lotion. Both were tanned to a chocolate-brown colour: one lay on his front, one on his back, together fitting snugly on a large, blue-and-white striped, square cotton sarong. In nothing but tiny swimming trunks and shades, the one on his front was chastising the other for rubbing suntan lotion in an 'aggressive' manner. The one doing the rubbing disputed the claim before slapping a hand full of the white sun cream down hard on his friend's thigh. 'Owww!' howled the recipient. 'That really hurt!'

Morning slipped into afternoon and as the cooler hours set in I moved out of the shade and into the sun. The beach was filling out with people. A young family arrived and slowly the mother, father and three children positioned themselves next to me in the sun. Towels, balls, buckets, spades, goggles, masks, sun cream, books, magazines and sunglasses tumbled out of bags onto the sand as the family settled into their spot. The mother had a large, green plastic, cool box from which she pulled out thick sandwiches, fruit and bottles of drink that she distributed to her hungry charges. She handed one sandwich to each child and they, in turn, took the large, floury slabs and ran off into the sunshine. Soon after, the father went for a swim leaving the mother sitting silent and alone. Her soft skin shone in the sun.

At one end of the promenade was a beach bar serving drinks and snacks. People filed to and fro and some settled at the tables out front, which were sheltered by the shade of four large palm trees. I bought a pastrami sandwich and a Coke from the bar and then returned to my spot, resting my back against the rough, peeling white paint on the old wooden frame of the lifeguard stand. While I tore hungrily through my late lunch I browsed the *Reader*. It's issued every Thursday morning and it's within the sections of the *Reader* that you can find yourself an apartment to buy or rent, restaurants and cafés to eat in, clubs and bars to visit, concerts and events to go to, records, books and clothes to buy. Where can I buy a second-hand car? Where can I find a lover? Check the *Reader*. When I first came to Chicago it was by scouring the 'accommodation' section of the *Reader* that I'd found my apartment. Now, feeling healthy and rested from a day on the beach, it was an evening's entertainment I was seeking in the free paper's pages.

I'd remembered Derrick Carter mentioning Slick's Lounge as one of the best clubs for house music in the city. Cajmere had also said that he goes to Slick's a lot when he's in town. I'd already sampled the local house music scene at the Red Dog – Monday is the official 'gay night' but just a good place to head for a blow-out whatever you're into – as well as the Crow Bar and Zanibar, to see Derrick play. Tuesday nights at Slick's was, according to the *Reader*, the night when local DJ Diz, who also has his own record label Igloo and makes records with his partner Iz for Derrick's Classic Records label, was DJing.

Slick's is in a part of town that's hard to define in terms of neighbourhoods. Set in a kind of industrial zone that doesn't really have a name, the best way to describe its location is that it lies somewhere in between what is now called Lincoln Park and my home neighbourhood Wicker Park.

The day I'd spoken to Duke, we'd discussed neighbourhoods and he'd told me that the culture of regeneration meant that certain areas in the city got 'abused' and that the bit of town known as Lincoln Park was one such abused place.

He described the area where Slick's operated as one of those places that has 'a real friendly "I can charge a lot more rent if I'm a building owner and I say my place is in Lincoln Park" kind of vibe' to it. Right next to an area called Logan Square – east of the highway but west of the Chicago River – it wasn't an area in its own right at all a few years ago. Since the area got gentrified about ten years ago, it just seemed to keep spreading. Duke's wife had grown up as a poor kid in that part of town but now if you want to live there you'd probably be charged $2,000 a month for a single-room apartment. Before the regeneration, he'd said, that was a cheap rent area where all the artists lived. It was also where you headed to buy a ten-dollar bag of heroin. Those pretty old houses that now cost 'through the roof' to live in, said Duke, used to be homes to 'poor black and Latino folk'.

'I guess the white folks just drove them out,' Duke had shrugged.

Right next to the Chicago River and just off the highway in this dark, desolate part of town with no real name of its own was where I ended up that night. Post Slick's, hot and sweaty from dancing to the sublime house music played through a crystal clear, loud-but-ear-friendly sound system, it was quite by chance I stumbled on a wooden shack of a drinking den nearby.

According to a scruffy-looking sign hanging over a few ramshackle tables and chairs outside the building, this hut was called the Hideout. The small window set in the front of the shack was steamed up as I approached, the glass thick with condensation blurring what was going on inside. Through that small, steamy oblong I could just make out, via the red glow of the lighting inside the building, a knees-up of a party; fuelled by what sounded like live oompah music. I went in and found a kooky three-piece band made up of guitar, double bass and washboard/vocalist.

The band were playing in the front room of this two-roomed bar to a crowd of about 30 people, who were drinking beers and dancing in a lively hoedown style. They were prancing from foot to foot, swinging each other around in circles, hopping up and down and back and forth and the only people not getting into the spirit of the jig were the handful of men at the bar. Sitting atop tall stools that lined the bar and nursing drinks served by the tall, blonde, curly-haired bartender, the focus of these drinkers was the rampant crowd. Made up of an equal mix of men and women, this trendy-looking throng were all going mad to the songs being belted out, unamplified, by this strange-looking trio.

The band, it turned out, was called Devil In A Woodpile. It was after their first set, throughout which I was transfixed as this urban barn dance got hotter, that I managed to corner the lead singer and jug/washboard player, Rick 'Cookin' Sherry. Pulling him away from the crowd was tough enough but once I did, and we were sitting in the empty backroom of the Hideout, I managed to ask him if he could try and describe exactly what it was that he'd been playing just minutes before.

'All the stuff we do, except for the few things we write, is kind of stuff from the Twenties, Thirties, Forties,' says Rick. 'It's classified as country blues but people get confused thinking that it's country music – especially because we're a bunch of white guys – but really it's blues. There was a big scene around the kind of music we play in the first half of the 20th century. The guys that started out playing this stuff were street musicians – in Memphis on Beale Street where a lot of guys from the South, out in the country, used to go out on the street and hustle. There was a big scene down there. The jug bands were just basically bands that had jug players in them, alongside harp, washboards and kazoo players. Probably the most famous one was The Memphis Jug Band. They made recordings and, as far as I'm concerned, they were basically a poor man's version of Duke Ellington as far as the arrangements went. They had some pretty cool stuff going on with harmonies and all this stuff. Except they were like a bunch of poor, country, black folks.

'This kind of music we base our sound on has basically just got this great soul. It's just got this driving rhythm and at the same time it had a lot of dynamics to it. A lot of songs varied. It was kind of on the verge of jazz and then hoedown blues. Then there was all the different sounds they got out of it. It was just really tight. It's just amazing compared to the type of music that's made today where it takes people three weeks to record a single song and it's going to be a pop hit because of all the over-dubbing and slick touches. As far as I'm concerned putting out pop music like that is like subconscious terrorism that they rip on your brain and make it stick, like a TV commercial. But these guys making the blues back then were recording this stuff with just one mic hanging in the middle of the room. That's a big part of it. I love it too because a lot of it is real humorous. It's funny stuff. At the same time they were – under the radar – slipping in some kind of political or socially relevant angle.'

On their most recent album *Division Street*, Devil In A Woodpile's songs cover topics like love and loss. There are both original songs and covers. Their version of Chicago blues man Big Bill Broonzy's 'Wrong Woman' is included. Just like artists making blues music in the city 50 years ago, the band get the inspiration for their country-themed music from everyday life.

'We basically should be categorised probably as a kind of a blues thing because we play blues. It's old blues but the thing is that it's not Chicago blues. Not in the sense of what that term actually means. I started out as a harmonica player and I don't know if it was in the back of my mind but I was looking for a different avenue as a harmonica player. There's a ton of guys here doing the Little-Walter-with-Muddy-Waters type thing but I didn't really want to do that. That stuff is so loud too. We're a blues band that doesn't really get hired to play in blues clubs. In Rosa's and Buddy Guys Legends, they'll hire the acoustic acts – Buddy's actually does early sets every Friday and Saturday so we get in there quite a bit for a happy-hour crowd.

'At the same time people don't really know how to describe us. There's a guy who called me and wants to hire me for a private party and he called us a "Dixieland Band". We get gigs around Mardi Gras and they think we're like a Mardi Gras, New Orleans thing. We get "blue grass" listed as us. We're none of that. But at the same time, what's cool is that we get a lot of bookings doing restaurant gigs. A rock player might look down at that. Like "these guys – they do frigging restaurant no-brainer gigs, in an old persons' home", but to us it's a regular gig and in this business anything regular is nice. We don't need any microphones, we're not too loud, but at the same time we're not boring or, on the other hand, "demanding of you to be listening to all our little lyrics" kind of band. For something like the Hideout we pump it out more than usual – more than in a restaurant gig for example where we don't want to shake the food out of people's mouths. They're eating so their hands and mouths are busy and we're not really going to get any applause. We're just in the background doing stuff; which is fine.

'When I'm planning in my head what we want to play, we don't really think of it in terms of a fixed set. We never do like a big rock show where we've got to spit out our music in, like, 30 minutes. That's why I don't do set lists or anything like that. I'm trying to mix it up. I was out last night at a local club and there was a really good country band playing. I've never been a huge fan of country music; I'm kind of ignorant of the stuff. But, you know, these guys are great players and stuff but I heard an hour of the same thing. Same singers, same kind of breaks and when I'm playing out a set I kind of try to say, "okay let's do a fast one, let's do a slow one, let's do a washboard one, let's get out the clarinet, let's get out the harp, let's take out the jug". It's all about fitting the mood of where you're playing.'

Rick describes what Devil In A Woodpile do down at the Hideout as their 'rock show' in the sense that the band rarely does live gigs to big audiences 'except for the few times' that they get booked to play rock clubs. The band has been doing Tuesday nights at the Hideout since 1997. Down there on Tuesday nights the band plays for tips. There's no cover charge at the Hideout, so a jar is sent round during the night and the crowd gets a chance to chip in. The bar offers the band a guarantee and most Tuesdays, says Rick, the band hits that with the tips. It's a fairly normal deal for bands that play in bars in the city that have no cover charge, says Rick, although it's taken a while to get used to as none of them are actually from Chicago.

'I'm from upstate New York,' he told me. 'The others are from out of town too. The thing we have in common is that we're all into this old blues sound. Another big influence for us, and you can see this in a lot of the washboard tunes we've covered, is a guy named

Washboard Sam. He was a real deltability man. His stuff is right out there. You're really going to be able to hear him when he plays and there's a lot of that in our music. He did a lot of recording in Chicago. He was one of these who came up from the South and a lot of the stuff we do is in that vein. Very upbeat, like a lot of the stuff recorded on the Bluebird label.'

Best known for its jazz output and releasing artists like Louis Armstrong, Duke Ellington, Glenn Miller and Artie Shaw, the Victor-affiliated Bluebird Records also put out blues records between the 1920s and 1950s. Notable blues men like Tampa Red, Big Bill Broonzy and Sonny Boy Williamson, who embodied the first blues explosion that hit Chicago in the 1930s, all recorded for the label. Bluebird was based in Chicago and run by local producer/A&R director Lester Melrose, who also arranged music for Columbia Records.

Many of the artists Melrose recorded had moved up from the South during the great migration and with them brought the blues music they'd play in their homes. This country blues sound, when set against an urban backdrop, soon started changing – and Melrose had a part in this transition. He opted for a band sound, setting each artist within this context. Guitars – acoustic and electric – were combined with piano, bass and a rhythm section often made up of drums and washboard. The style of recordings that emerged from these Melrose-arranged groups and that got released on Bluebird Records was later dubbed 'Bluebird beat'. It was the first, distinctive Chicago blues sound.

'If you look at what the roots of Devil In A Woodpile are, then we pull a lot of stuff out of there,' says Rick. 'The Sonny Boy, "Good Morning School Girl" kind of stuff and Big Bill Broonzy's "Keep On Drinking". These guys are the guys that kind of evolved from the solo-esque guitar players out on the street corners to jug bands where they're starting to deal with ensembles. That's when those guys started moving up to Chicago. This was pre-Muddy Waters – this was the 1940s. At the end of Prohibition, clubs were opening up all over the place and you'd get these bands that were bringing it all together. You had a harp player, a piano player, a bass – they did a lot of recording in Chicago on the Bluebird label. So that's where a lot of that comes from and that was still unplugged. No one was playing through an amplifier. Kind of at the edge of the 1940s you could hear some of the stuff where Big Bill Broonzy's amped up and stuff like that. Harmonica players weren't using the little bullet microphones to get the distorted kind of sound. That's where a lot of it comes from.'

Bluebird Records defined the sound of blues music coming out of Chicago during the 1930s until, later that decade and in the early 1940s, the music became infused with jazz and took on a more 'jump up' blues sound. That peppier version of the 12-bar, three-chord style of blues would become solidified after Muddy Waters, also known as McKinley Morganfield, arrived in the city.

Muddy moved up to Chicago from Mississippi in the early 1940s. He'd been playing the guitar and singing his deep bottom blues music in Mississippi's Delta region for nearly a decade before he made it to the city. In Chicago, he would hang out and play on Maxwell Street. This market, on the corner of Maxwell and Halsted, was of special importance to Chicago's music scene during the great migration. Newly arrived musicians from the rural South would bring their guitars and harmonicas down to Maxwell Street where they could jam and meet other musicians. The market was alive with smells and sounds in those days and was, in a way, a replica of what life had been like in the South. Preachers would come to Maxwell Street to preach the Word. Hustlers would peddle 'illegals' in between the sausage and pork chop stands. Add to this the jazz and blues music that was played down there by street musicians – all hoping for their big break – and it's no surprise that John Landis chose Maxwell Street for selected scenes in his 1980s movie *The Blues Brothers*. It was to Maxwell Street that Muddy first came to play when he arrived in the city and, from the connections he made there, he eventually managed to group together enough musicians for a band.

It was Muddy Waters and his band that brought the amplified sound to blues music and to widespread audiences in the late 1940s and early 1950s. His band, cobbled together from musicians he met in and around the city, was the catalyst that kick-started the sound of Chicago blues as we know it today.

When Muddy moved to Chicago, he hooked up with local label Chess Records and it was Muddy's music, especially his electric blues sound, that became the label's signature sound at the time. His singing style was to hang slightly behind the beat, forcing the musicians with whom he played to drive the rhythm forward. He played the guitar with a strong emphasis on the second and fourth beats in the bar. This wasn't a style he had invented, but it was through Muddy, and the success he would enjoy after he moved to Chicago, that the sound became popularised. This rhythm – that marked a new phase to blues music when Muddy started pounding it out in the late 1940s and early 1950s – would become the backbone of the Chicago blues sound. It was this rhythmic pattern that would also, less than a decade after Muddy popularised it, pump out the first heartbeat of rock'n'roll.

The legacy of Muddy Waters' electric guitar sound sits at the root of much of the blues music that is played in the city today. But for Devil In A Woodpile, playing unplugged lies at the heart of the music they make. According to Rick it was that idea that prompted them to take up the gig at the Hideout in 1997. At the time they just saw it as an opportunity to play regularly, little realising that an entire mini-scene would spring up around their Tuesday night hoedowns. It's those weekly events that have been running since, and that have made the name of the Hideout as a trendy hang-out spot. More importantly, the weekly Devil In A Woodpile gigs have turned a subsection of Chicago's young music fans onto a strain of the blues that was previously unknown. As far as Rick is concerned, the whole thing has happened by accident.

'The Hideout is like a hip little club and when we started there we were like the first musical act those guys hired,' he says. 'We were kind of looking for a little hole-in-the-wall kind of place where we could just sit and play unplugged and kind of practise our stuff. We walked into the place when they were still putting tiles on the floor. The Hideout kind of blew up in a big way, popularity-wise. For us it was just like an excuse to get together but the whole thing kind of took off in a way that we weren't expecting. We like it but we were really looking for a little place that probably wasn't going to have music and we were like a special little thing. In the beginning it was kind of like we were the pioneer discoverers of a cool, new bar and a lot of real hip people came to check it out. It's kind of gone through all that now, but lots of people still turn up. There have been all these write-ups on the place and our Tuesday night gigs there but nowadays I hardly know anyone in there. My old buddies aren't coming up too often – they turn up once in a blue moon. It's kind of a young crowd that's really loud and it's really like you got to work your ass to get some tips out of them.'

Devil In A Woodpile are signed to Bloodshot Records, a local independent label that's also home to stars like Ryan Adams and maverick, alternative country band The Waco Brothers. Since it started up in 1993, Bloodshot Records has been at the epicentre of an 'alternative country' revolution in America. Rick insists he has no idea what the term 'alt country' actually means, but if you read magazines like *No Depression* or UK style magazine *The Face*, then you'll find a certain look that formed around the scene in 2003. Dungarees came back in vogue for the first time since the 1980s. This hillbilly look permeated the catwalk and then the High Street at the time. Hype aside, though, it's Chicago, via Bloodshot, that is one of the alt-country hot spots in terms of a supporting live music scene. The music itself is based around the bones of old school white American folk music, or country and western music, but with the added injection of the punk ethic of challenging lyrics and sassy, insurgent themes. Devil In A Woodpile, according to Rick, are 'at one extreme of what those guys do' and not really typical of the rest of the label's output. In terms of the music they make, their sound is unique: a strain of blues music that hasn't been seen or heard in America for decades. The band might all now be based in Chicago, and what they play and record might well be blues music. But, says Rick, that's as far as the comparison goes.

'It's Chicago blues but we're not like 1950s – the big, big sound that gave Chicago the name of "home of the blues",' says Rick. For a record label more in tune with the traditional Chicago blues sound, Rick said, I should look up Alligator Records.

THE JOURNEY up to Edgewater, in the far North Side of the city where Alligator is based, is a long one if you're taking a cab from the near West Side in mid-week, rush-hour traffic.

'We're going right to the edge of Chicago, right by Evanston,' said the cab driver when I asked him the route. Evanston, I remembered from speaking to Duke, was the 'fancy' suburb of Chicago; the city-hugging, suburban area that was home to a largely white, middle-class brand of Chicago people.

Driving through the traffic, with the sun beating down outside, I tried to dredge up what I could remember about Alligator Records from my conversation with Rick a few days earlier. The label, owned and run by Bruce Iglauer, started up in 1970, just after the second blues explosion that hit Chicago in the Sixties. Blues had only attracted black music fans up until the 1950s when white musicians started getting influenced by the sound. The first generation of white rock musicians, characterised by bands like The Rolling Stones who emerged in the early 1950s, always paid allegiance to their blues influences – but blues music at this time still attracted a mainly black audience of listeners. It wasn't until the 1960s, off the back of the folk music craze that hit America, that a white audience got into the blues. Iglauer was one of them.

He had got turned onto the blues while at college and had moved to Chicago after graduating, in order to be close to the musicians, bars and clubs in the city that played the music that he loved. Artists like Muddy Waters, Sonny Stitt and Little Walter were all playing in Chicago and servicing the thriving scene that earned the city the name 'home of the blues'. Iglauer got a job working at local label Delmark Records, which was run by record store owner and ardent blues fan Bob Koester. As shipping clerk at Delmark, Iglauer got to sit in on recording sessions with artists like harmonica player Junior Wells and soon picked up a taste for what it was to run and manage a record label and record artists in and from the city.

Iglauer arrived in Chicago in 1967 and three years later he started Alligator Records. The first artist he recorded was guitarist/singer Hound Dog Taylor, a local musician whom Iglauer wanted Koester to record as a Delmark artist. Koester didn't want to do it, so Iglauer did.

Since then, he's recorded some of the most successful blues artists in the US. The brilliant Fenton Robinson released two albums through Alligator. Son Seals made a string of recordings for the label. Chicago's 'queen of the blues' Koko Taylor has been with Alligator Records since the late Seventies and remains one of the imprint's most successful and highest-selling artists. In terms of the jump-up Chicago blues sound that the city is known for, it is Alligator Records that is home to the group of artists directly responsible for keeping the sound alive in the city. Chicago guitarist-singer Lil' Ed Williams plays two or three times a week in the city with his Blues Imperial band. Lonnie Brooks is another Chicago blues man whose output is released by Alligator and he plays regularly in the city too.

As the head of one of the city's prominent independent labels, Bruce Iglauer is a man with strong views on the Chicago blues scene.

'When I came to Chicago, Muddy Waters was pushing 60 years old,' says Iglauer, as he sits behind the oblong desk in his office. 'Blues is associated with an old culture. It is a healing music. You listen to the blues to get rid of the blues. It's about tension and release. It's about feeling that other people are sharing in the things that are bugging you.

'Chicago has become a mecca for blues tourists, and a lot of people who come here even in tour groups think "I should have a night of authentic Chicago music". So you get clubs like the two Blue Chicago clubs, which are very definitely tourist-oriented and they're so tourist-oriented that Gino Pataglio who runs them, who's a really good guy, says that every band that he has in has to include a black, female singer. He'll also tell the singer to go out into the crowd and ask if there's anyone in from New York, LA, wherever else. They're good because they keep a lot of musicians working but they feed into the blues clichés. The leading blues club in Chicago is undoubtedly Buddy Guy's Legends, which has been here for close to 15 years now. I had my wedding reception there. It's pretty grotty but the music is good.

'There's another blues audience which is a black blues audience which is a blue collar, often Southern-born or Southern-rooted, maybe still living in the South audience, which is very heavily female. They tend to listen to the artists they grew up on like Little Milton, Bobby

Bland, Denise Lasalle, the late Johnny Taylor, Bobby Rush – that's the kind of blues that's heard on black radio stations that play the blues these days. The black female audience is still a very important part of the black, ghetto blues scene here in the city and these ladies are generally pretty adult because they grew up with blues. But the blues stopped being fashionable in the black community some years ago. So these are people who keep the interest in the blues going.

'I think that a lot of my audience, unfortunately for me, have aged with me. One of the reasons I've been a success is that I figured out there are a lot of people just like me who wanted to know more about blues and hear more blues. When I say just like me, I mean my age, my sex – primarily because a huge number of the white blues fans are men. Maybe because the music has this macho thing going on too.'

Iglauer's office is cram-packed full of CDs and records, some still stuffed in the bubble-wrap package-mailers in which they were no doubt delivered. The walls are covered with posters, pictures, discs and flyers. Posters of Alligator artists Koko Taylor, Fenton Robinson and Lonnie Brooks bear down onto this dark, top-floor room that's distinguishable from the others in this three-storey building because it's stuffed full of alligators. Large, plastic ones, ceramic ones, soft alligator toys and rubber alligators cover every surface of the office. On the large desk, the low coffee table, the filing cabinets, sofa and mantelpiece, alligators of all shapes and sizes sit beady-eyed and quiet.

The label is called Alligator Records because that's Bruce's nickname, a tag he was given because of his habit of gnashing his teeth to the drum parts in records. It's not the only quirk to this man. Minutes after meeting him, Bruce rushes over to his briefcase and pulls out a tape cassette of blues artist Mississippi Fred McDowell's *Mississippi Delta Blues* album. It was after hearing Fred McDowell play his country blues sound at a folk festival one summer, that Bruce got turned onto the form. The *Mississippi Delta Blues* album was the first blues record that Bruce bought and he hasn't looked back since. Admitting to being 'a little superstitious', it's an album without which Bruce never leaves home. He has a very specific reason for this: if, all of a sudden, he were in a situation where his 'number was about to come up', he'd be able to go out listening to his favourite blues star.

'I carry that cassette so that if I'm on a flight and the plane begins to plunge earthwards and I know I've got 30 seconds to live – I can grab that cassette and slap it on and go out with Fred. Just like I came in with Fred,' says Bruce.

It's that same life dedication to blues music that Bruce applies to Alligator Records. It all started for him at the age of 18, when he left his hometown of Cincinnati to go to a folk festival upstate.

'You know that scene in the movies where someone becomes hysterical and the hero grabs them by the shirt and slaps them a couple of times? Then the person ceases being hysterical and says something silly like "thanks, I needed that". Well, when Fred McDowell, from 20 rows away, shot that music out to me, it grabbed me by the collar and slapped me around the face and I said "thanks, I needed that". It was as though everything I'd been listening to, up until that time, was false and plastic. And removed from reality. What I heard that day was such first-person music. It was a man singing about his own life, and not a life that he as a suburban person imagined himself in, but a life he was actually living even at that point. Here's a guy who was at a folk festival and the next week he's pumping gas outside of a Stuckies Restaurant in Mississippi. And playing parties on weekends. I was energised and exhilarated and my eyes and ears were opened, and maybe my soul was opened.'

When Bruce arrived in Chicago in the 1960s, most of the blues music in the city was based in the South Side. The Chicago blues scene then was a black scene, unwritten about and unreported on in the white-run, local press. According to Bruce, there was a brief North Side Chicago blues scene in the late Sixties when the Paul Butterfield Blues Band got together. It was around the Rush Street/Wells Street area where the now closed Fickle Pickle and some other folk clubs booked some blues artists. Then that scene vanished.

Bruce remembers a piano player called Bob Reidy, who'd come from Wisconsin and started a blues band. He got a gig at the Wise

Fools Pub on 2270 North Lincoln Avenue, and he began bringing single black artists to be guests with his band. Johnny Young, John Littlejohn, Koko, Lonnie Brooks and a few others were all booked to play. Bob actually encouraged Jimmy Rodgers, who'd played in Muddy Waters's band, to come out of retirement. Then he established a circuit of three or four other clubs in the city – all North Side clubs – where his band would play. He'd play four or five nights a week. The result was that he had to bring in other bands to fill in when he couldn't do it. The next thing you know, says Bruce, there were black blues bands in three or four places in the North Side.

This happened around 1971–72. Bob then went on to record a couple of albums. He played as a sideman on a session for an Alligator Records recording. Then he got into 'some trouble'. He disappeared and he's been gone ever since but in his wake he left the North Side of Chicago with a fully functioning blues scene. The clubs that were taking on black blues bands were making money with the blues. An old coffee house called Kingston Mines started booking blues bands and that eventually became one of the most important blues clubs in the city. It still is. The Mines is right across the street from B.L.U.E.S. on Halsted. Today, that area of town plays host to local blues bands like the Alligator-signed Lil' Ed and The Blues Imperials.

Ed grew up on the West Side of Chicago which enjoyed its own flourishing blues scene in the 1950s. Much of the early Chicago blues had been played on the South Side of the city but, by the 1950s, black neighbourhoods had stretched to the West Side of Chicago. The blues music that was played in the neighbourhood bars around the West Side of the city was funkier than the South Side blues, and more attuned to the style of blues legend BB King.

Local West Side blues men like JB Hutto played this peppier, funkier blues brand in the area. Hutto, alongside other local blues men like Sunnyland Slim, Walter Horton and JB Lenior, all played and recorded on city-based labels Cobra and Chance. Cobra Records was a short-lived imprint based in Chicago's West Side that followed in the trail blazed by Chess Records. Guitarist Otis Rush recorded a string of sides for Cobra, as did another West Side guitarist-vocalist named

Magic Sam. By the mid–late 1950s, the West Side blues scene was almost as vibrant as the blues scene on the South Side of Chicago. Lil' Ed grew up listening to the music played in bars around the West Side. JB Hutto was his uncle so he had an 'in' to gigs that other kids his age could never swing.

Ed's style of blues remains faithful to this West Side tradition. His sound is a raucous, jump-up blues that he and his band play loud and amplified nearly every weekend in the city. If you pay the $10 cover charge at B.L.U.E.S. on Halsted on a Saturday night, the people you'll encounter are the ones who buy Bruce's output on Alligator Records. The crowd is distinctly middle-aged and mostly white. Tourists frequent the blues clubs in this area. If you go and see Ed play, you'll find a stack of out-of-towners queuing up at the end of the gig to buy one of his CDs that his wife sells at the front of the stage. Next to that you'll find another queue of people who've just bought CDs waiting for Ed to sign them.

Ed's music covers themes that have long been covered in music: love, heartache, women, drinking, money. It's party music. In terms of blues, it's reminiscent of a style that's been around for over half a century. Lil' Ed is one of the bestselling artists on Bruce's Alligator Records but, according to Bruce, Alligator Records' style of Chicago blues isn't all about looking back.

'I don't think it's just a nostalgia thing at all,' says Bruce. 'I think that the emotional message keeps coming through. I think a lot of people who know nothing about the tradition can still feel the music. I think the feeling in the music comes first. Why did Fred McDowell, who had nothing in common with me, speak so loudly to me? Because the emotional message was so strong that it cut through the fact that he literally couldn't read and write and grew up farming in overalls. It was assumed when I was born that I'd have a college education and it was assumed when he was born that he'd be a share cropper. How come he could speak to me? Because the music is stronger than just being a part of culture.

'However, I do think the blues will have to change if it's going to survive. The blues, in order to make it, has to speak clearly and relevantly to a current, contemporary audience. It has to have the emotional function of blues, which is that healing thing. That "it hurts so good" thing. That "wringing you out like a wet wash cloth" thing. The tension and release.

'I think this is a very crucial time for the blues. Because unlike any other form of music, we're in a situation, with the blues, where the icon of blues BB King – the only nationally known living blues musician – is 77 years old. When BB is no longer able to perform, or dies, a lot of people are going to say, "well, the blues is dead". If this music, and the emotional healing that is so much a part of this music, is going to survive, then new blues artists need to work out how to speak to contemporary audiences. They have to try to carry this tradition forward in some way. I'm trying to nurture the artists who are going to do that. There are young people making blues music, but there aren't enough of them. One thing that happens when you get into the blues world is that your definition of young changes.'

Lil' Ed is considered 'young' for a blues artist and he is 50 years old. Blues music as created by Ed is still urban folk music but its themes are only relevant to an older generation of urban folk. Head down into the rougher parts of Chicago's South Side and the 'it hurts so good' theme doesn't seem so relevant any more. The rougher parts of Chicago contribute to the city having one of the highest levels of gun crime of any city in America. 'Tension and release', as understood by Bruce Iglauer, means something entirely different to young, urban folk surviving life in Chicago's ghetto today. In terms of black, urban, folk music it's the harshly real lyrics in rap, not blues music, that speak to young people living in cities today. Blues music is mostly supported and listened to by white audiences, while rap has become the neighbourhood music of young African-Americans. Today, rap serves the same purposes that blues did back then: telling stories, examining the culture, relaying news. Young, urban, black folk living in the ghetto aren't just blue, they're angry. Blues clubs and bars across Chicago are packed full of people swigging beer, dancing, and singing along to the classic blues songs that got them through the ups and downs in their lives. But on the streets of Chicago, young people are living those times out, all the while carefully crafting a new soundtrack that will hopefully help to guide them through life.

WHATEVER kind of day it is in the city, whatever time of day you fancy seeing it, one of the best views of Chicago's immense skyline can be taken from right in the heart of it all, downtown at the intersection of State and Madison. It's here that the Chicago River slices a path clean through the tall buildings, dividing the city's heaving downtown Loop area into two tidy sections. Stand on any of the 19 bridges that join the two parts of town and you can see Chicago's lofty, artificial heart in all its fully functioning and glittering glory. On a sunny day, the sleek skyscrapers reach the sky with the grace and beauty of fairytale turrets, cool and proud in the desiccating heat. At the base of these smooth sentries, the daytime traffic that buzzes in the streets of the main downtown area (that extends about 16 blocks south and about seven blocks north of the Chicago River's main channel) can seem oddly insignificant.

It is the fast-flowing river itself, and not the roads that surround and cross it, that is the most fitting boundary to this district of skyscrapers. On a winding stretch of this wide river, small speedboats and larger cruisers snake their leisurely path through the heart of the city. A handful of cruise companies offer trips along this glitzy stretch of river. Going from the artificial North Shore Channel that pulls water from Lake Michigan at Wilmette Harbor before flowing south through the Pilsen area on 16th Street, these tourist-heavy boats then head downtown. They drift past the Wrigley Building, the IBM Plaza and the Merchandise Mart, then make their way south before turning round and cruising back again.

It's certainly a wonderful way for any visitor or resident to experience this part of the city. But I enjoyed the river most by standing on solid ground, stock still in the middle of one of the bridges, grasping tight onto the ledge and looking down onto the water. Like most urban rivers, the Chicago River sweeping through the tall cityscape is normally a murky grey, in sharp contrast to the gaily lit flotilla that bobs on its waters. Only on St Patrick's Day each year, when the river is dyed bottle green for the occasion, is there any change to this rule. Each time I found myself standing looking down at the dusky water racing below, I had a sense of time moving fast; unstoppable and directly in tune with the elements.

The Chicago River originates north of the city in Lake County and flows south until it joins the Desplaines River; and it was on the margins of this river that Chicago first began to take shape hundreds of years ago. Although life has continued to change rapidly around it, the river itself has been quietly constant.

From above, the river can be seen to form a wonky Y shape, with its shortest, eastern fork joining Lake Michigan. It's 156 miles long, it meanders through 24 Chicago neighbourhoods – and it's worth remembering that it was the river that gave its name to the city and not the other way round. It's a compass of sorts, too: one of the best ways to navigate Chicago is to remember that Lake Michigan is always to the east and that it's actually the river that forms the most important division in the city.

The very first inhabitants of the land surrounding Chicago were the Potawatomi Indians who, when they pitched up there in the 16th century, called the area 'Chicagau', meaning 'place of wild onion or garlic', both of which grew in abundance in that area at the time. After the Potawatomi, the Miami, Shawnee, Ottawa, Delaware, Iroquois and Chippewa tribes all made their homes along the banks of the river and while people and generations that made their homes in the area shifted, the name 'Chicagau' stuck.

It was the first European explorers – French Canadian Louis Joliet and Father Jacques Marquette who came to the area in 1673 and 1674 respectively – who changed the name of the area from 'Chicagau' to 'Chicago'. But it wasn't until over a hundred years later that Chicago had its first permanent settlers.

When Haitian explorer Jean Baptiste Pointe Du Sable rolled up in the late 18th century, it was the Chicago River that he and his companies used to help transform the area into a proper settlement. When US Federal Troops built Fort Dearborn in 1802, the city finally began to take shape and the Chicago River, leading from Lake County in the north down south to Mississippi became an important expressway of the time. Used for the travel, shipping and navigation that were essential for building a centre for trade, commerce and industry, Chicago became, and remains today, one of the most important cities in the Western world.

If you stand on the bridge where the three divisional forks of the Chicago River meet, you are literally at point zero in terms of Chicago's grid system.

This spot, at the intersection of State and Madison and in the heart of the Loop, is, as far as geographical layout goes, the centre of the city. From here, State Street divides east and west and Madison divides north and south. Numbered streets in the city run from east to west getting higher as you travel from north to south beginning at 12th Street, which is also known as Roosevelt Road. East–west streets north of Madison, and all north–south streets, have names instead of numbers and the first few streets south of Madison are known as the Presidents, because they are named after US presidents in order of their terms. Former presidents Madison, Monroe, Adams, Jackson, Van Buren, Polk and Taylor are honoured in this way.

Not far from this spot, near the corner of Adams Street and Michigan Avenue, is a sign that reads 'Begin Historic Route 66', the beginning of one of the world's most famous roads. Also close by, a mere five-minute stroll away, is one of the city's most important musical landmarks. There are no street signs to point the way and not every city worker buzzing around the area will know how to direct you there if you ask them; but if you make your way to Wabash Street, you'll find jazz/blues record store the Jazz Record Mart, which is owned by Bruce Iglauer's former boss and Delmark Records' founder Bob Koester.

Delmark Records as a label, individual releases from that imprint - namely Magic Sam's 'West Side Solo' record – and even Bob Koester himself have all been appointed to the blues Hall Of Fame over the years. In 2003 Delmark enjoyed its 50th anniversary, making it one of the world's longest-running independent jazz/blues labels. If you take time scouring the innards of the Jazz Record Mart, you'll find nearly every single release that's been put out through Delmark for sale on the shelves or in the bins. Any Delmark release you can't find is likely to be packed tight into the shelves of the stock room out back of the store. All you have to do is ask one of Bob's members of staff, or Bob himself, and they'll probably find what you're looking for within minutes.

The Record Mart has been on Wabash Street for the past seven years. Before that the shop was located just round the corner on Grand Avenue. It was at this 750ft sq location, back in the late Sixties, that Bruce Iglauer had shown up when he first arrived in the city. He had gotten a tip-off from a Canadian folk magazine called *Hoot* that he'd picked up at a folk festival in Canada in the summer of 1966 and in those pages – he still has that very same copy – he had read a review of some blues LPs due out on Chicago's Chess Records.

At the very end of the review, Bruce remembered, was an inscription that read something like this: 'If you're ever in Chicago and you want to hear some of this music live, then go to the Jazz Record Mart at 7 West Grand and Bob Koester will take you out to the clubs in the Chicago ghetto where this music is played.'

Bruce arrived in Chicago in the summer of 1967, went down to the Jazz Record Mart on 7 West Grand and met Bob Koester, who took him out to some blues clubs in the South Side of the city. The next day Bruce went back to the Jazz Record Mart and asked Bob for a job. He was offered the $30 a week post as shipping clerk for Delmark Records and Bruce moved to Chicago for good the following week.

The Jazz Record Mart stayed at 7 West Grand for a good number of years before moving to its present site on 444 N Wabash. In the 50 or so years since the label started and the 40 or so years since the Jazz Record Mart first opened its doors, Chicago has changed a great deal – not just the city itself but also the music scene around it. But one thing that hasn't changed, according to Bruce Iglauer and just about any other Chicago jazz or blues fan I came across during my stay in the city, is Bob Koester himself.

So it was after one of my head-cleansing, soul-soothing, solitary moments looking down at the timeless rush of the Chicago River early one afternoon that I decided to make a trip to the Jazz Record Mart to see if I could corner Koester for a chat.

Independent record stores all over the world are the same: they share a conspiratorial quiet. They are quiet in the sense that no one is really talking, as opposed to an actual silence. There's usually music playing when you enter an independent record store, but aside of that it's the absence of human chatter that makes record shopping in an independent store an almost spiritual experience. Forget the convenience of chains like HMV, Tower and Virgin for a moment and there's nothing that compares to the feeling of walking into an independent, specialist record store. The minute you walk through the door you get that sense of possibility, of history and of calm as you observe the individuals quietly flicking through the shelves. Whenever I've been record shopping, wherever I've been doing it, I've always found that weekday afternoons are the best time for it. It's at this time of day that the areas surrounding the aisles, shelves and bins of any record store are uncluttered and free for browsing and this was exactly how I found the Jazz Record Mart when I walked in that afternoon.

The entrance to the Jazz Record Mart is under a covered walkway, at the top of a small flight of stairs. Here a glass-fronted door opens up into a large room filled with vertical rows of racks, all storing vinyl, CDs and tapes. The boxed-off till area by the left of the front door has a few racks stationed around it holding magazines, postcards, t-shirts and rolled-up posters. To the right of the door is a stack of the latest issues of the *Reader*, just like there are in most record stores and bars around the city, as well as the store's self-published, freebie mag *Rhythm & News*. Just past the till on the left-hand wall of the vast main room is an arch leading through to a smaller anteroom. Here there are listening stations, shelves of vinyl positioned horizontally and vertically and a large desk topped with stacks of unpriced vinyl and sleeveless 78s. Beyond the desk on the far wall of the room are the doors of the stock room and another room. It is in this second room, sitting at a large, cluttered, wooden desk covered in various-sized piles of records and CDs, that I catch my first sight of Bob Koester. I move over to the door and just as I'm about to open my mouth and introduce myself to Bob, a customer – aged about 55 years old and clutching an inch-thick pile of vinyl under his arm – beats me to it with a question.

'You got any Caruso 78s in here?' the man asks Bob.

'I got some right over there,' says Bob, lifting his head from the pile of papers he's reading and motioning towards a two-foot-high pile of sleeveless 78s stacked on a table in the corner of the second room in the store. Bob gets up slowly and shuffles away from the desk, out of the back room and towards the stack of 78s.

'He was the Elvis of his day you know,' continues Bob as the man follows close behind him.

As this grey-haired, grey-bearded old man makes his way back to the back-room desk, I manage to introduce myself and before long, we are chatting. Bob continues to work as we talk, shuffling over to a shelf in the back corner of the smaller room in the shop to sort through a pile of Columbia 78s, wipe them down, put them in new sleeves, price them up and shelve them.

'You see if the red label on one of these Columbia 78s has gold print on it, then it must be pre-war,' explains Bob, holding up a thick, black, heavy-grooved shellac disc and showing me the type on the dark red, round label in the centre. The artist is Harry James and his name and the title of the record are indeed printed in thick, gilt type. It was during World War Two, he explains, that the US government announced that metallic ink could no longer be used on labels and signs. Bob knows these facts because he has lived through the times he talks about. He is now aged 70 and he has, so he tells me, lived and worked his whole life with music.

He was born in St Louis in the early 1930s and it was there that he started getting a taste for traditional jazz and early blues music. He started collecting and trading records while still at high school and opened his first record store in St Louis in 1952, just a year before he started Delmark Records.

Costing $40 a month to rent, Bob's first store held about 1,000 78s, ranging from blues to bebop and including newer releases alongside records from the 1920s by artists like Ma Rainey and Blind Lemon

Jefferson; both of whom released through Paramount Records. Back then the shop was nothing but a small, sweaty little room positioned on 3549 McCleave Street, just round the corner from Bob's dorm room at St Louis University. The space didn't have air-conditioning – it hadn't become a household commodity by then – and in high summer the temperatures soared way into the hundreds. At such times, business would, remembers Bob, 'turn to shit'. During the summer Bob would close the store and spend the hot months from July through to September accumulating vinyl to sell in his shop the following autumn.

Bob started Delmark Records because he wanted to record a local Dixieland band called The Windy City Six. He made the recording in 1953 and issued it as a 10-inch LP the following year. Back then the label was actually called 'Delmar', a name that referred to the corner of two St Louis streets called Delmar and Oliver. The intersection of these two streets marked the headquarters of as many as six or seven different St Louis jazz clubs, including the Windermere and the Barrel. At the Windermere, Bob caught his early tastes of the trad jazz sound that he loved while the Barrel played host to the bebop jazz players that came into town. It was at the Barrel that Bob saw Miles Davis and Albert Nicholas play. Back then, though, Bob admits that 'the avant garde jazz stuff went pretty much over my head'.

By the mid-Fifties, live jazz music was all over in St Louis but the clubs were way behind in terms of race relations. St Louis' clubs and bars were still under tight colour restrictions in those days and Bob remembers clubs like the Top Hat – a venue that played both traditional and modern jazz – only hiring white talent to play because they didn't want any blacks in the club. It was the same in bars and restaurants across the city.

'You never knew quite where you could take your black friends to dinner,' says Bob.

In 1959 Bob moved himself and his business to Chicago and took over a record store called Seymour's Record Mart on 444 North Wabash. By that time Delmar had become Delmark Records and Bob ran his label and his store at that site until 1962 before moving the operation to 7 West Grand. The shop at 7 West Grand was nothing but a storefront that was probably 20 feet wide and maybe 60/70 feet long. Bruce Iglauer remembers the place was 'filthy'. The walls were covered in green, institutional paint that you might see in a school cafeteria. There was dust on every available surface and in the free space were wooden bins with LPs and tables stacked high with 78s.

Delmark was set up in the basement. According to Bruce there was a big trapdoor that you would open to go downstairs to the basement, which was probably six and a half or seven feet high. There were roaches and mice. Two big wooden tables – one of which was Bob's desk and the other of which was the shipping table where Bruce worked. In one corner of the room was a cot where blues man Big Joe Williams slept when he came to Chicago. There were a lot of shelving units and later a shrink-wrap machine.

A few years later, Bob moved the Jazz Record Mart a couple of doors down on West Grand. It was now the late Sixties and by that time the jazz and blues scenes in Chicago were going through something of a renaissance, although each scene had its base in a separate area of the city. Jazz music was thriving on the North Side, while the popular live blues scene was largely restricted to the South Side 'ghetto' area of the city. By that time Muddy Waters' band had already had a string of hits out through local label Aristocrat Records. Aristocrat, a label run by Polish brothers Leonard and Phil Chess, was dissolved in 1950 and the brothers launched Chess Records that same year. By the mid-Fifties, Chess had put out a few blues compilation albums featuring tracks by local artists. Most of the local Chicago blues bands were already recording but they were only setting singles to wax and releasing them as 45s to the R&B market. It was Delmark that actually released the first studio-recorded blues artist album via Junior Wells' *Hoodoo Man Blues*.

Wells had been the harmonica player in Muddy Waters's band in the early 1950s, having joined when he was only 18. In the Chicago tradition, Wells played for the first time with Muddy's band when he joined them for a one-off at the Ebony Lounge, a club on West Chicago Avenue.

He had already made himself a name around town fronting a band called The Aces and doing session slots at gigs with some of the older bands around the city, and the rambunctious drive in his playing grabbed Muddy by the throat that night. It wasn't long before Wells was a permanent fixture in the band. By this time Little Walter Jacobs, Muddy's original harmonica player, had left the band to pursue other avenues. Because they didn't want to dilute the winning formula, however, Leonard and Phil Chess insisted that Little Walter continued to play harmonica whenever Muddy's band went into the Chess Studios to record. As a result Wells' name doesn't appear on the Muddy Waters's band recordings in the early Fifties, even though he was playing all the live gigs that the band performed in the city. Wells managed to actually record one session with Muddy's band before he was drafted into the military in the late 1950s. Bob Koester hooked up with Wells on the other side of his army stint.

'Recording *Hoodoo Man Blues* was a direct cause for Vanguard Records to sign Junior Wells,' says Koester. 'Delmark Records was only ever a starting point for artists. That's all I could ever promise an artist. I can't promise fame and fortune. I got so I could just about promise a trip to Europe for blues artists because European promoters used to give some respect to the people that we'd record. And what a starting point it was.'

Delmark Records' stint of blues recordings in the 1950s and 1960s helped kick-start the second blues explosion in the city. Playing in Junior Wells's band for the Delmark recording of *Hoodoo Man Blues* was a young guitarist named Buddy Guy, who is now Chicago's best-known blues export and the owner of one of the city's best blues clubs, Buddy Guy's Legends on 754 S Wabash. Bob actually signed Buddy Guy once but Buddy took both copies of the contract home to show his wife and Vanguard Records signed him the next day.

In 1967 Bob went into the studio to record the first Magic Sam record for Delmark. During that session Bob asked Magic Sam to record an almost unknown song called 'Sweet Home Chicago'. By 1971 or 1972, when Mighty Joe Young wanted to record that song, Bob had to say 'no, that's too well known a song'.

Bob's philosophy of getting musicians like Junior Wells and Magic Sam in to record what were basically club sets, brought blues songs that weren't necessarily fresh and new on the city's South Side scene to a whole new audience of listeners. Bob would also give artists the freedom to record fresh material they had written and it was this combination of the old and new that allowed blues music to permeate into popular culture.

Ask Bob Koester what he loves the most about the blues though, and he'll tell you it's the lyrics.

'It's the poetry of it that I love,' says Koester, as he picks out another old 78, dusts it down, finds a sleeve for it, prices it up and re-shelves it. 'I'm not too crazy about the music so much as the words. It's the kind of poetry I understand. It's just about basic things in life. You don't find kids who haven't hit puberty listening to blues because they haven't had the pressure that sex puts upon you in your adolescence. One of my gripes is that these days everyone is interested in the guitar licks in blues music and not the piano playing or the singing, but that's just like someone going to the opera and only listening to the orchestra. Some of the most revered blues artists are primarily singers and not even very good guitar players. Artists like Muddy Waters and Howlin' Wolf are prime examples. Muddy was a good enough guitar player but he was, primarily, a singer. That's why he was so good. It was the way he projected his voice. Buddy Guy is a hell of a singer too. I would have trouble telling if I like Buddy more than Magic Sam but I think I would say yes, as a singer. Buddy may be a better guitar player but I don't think in terms of guitar playing.'

Buddy Guy's Legends remains one of the most popular blues clubs in the city and one of the only regular blues haunts that lies outside of the North Side blues club circuit. The South Side, which was formerly a hotbed for the blues, is now stagnant in terms of live blues music. Blues music these days, says Bob, isn't blue collar music like it was in the 1930s and 1940s. According to him, young white folk who listen to blues don't have the same kind of money troubles that black urban blues fans had during those post-depression times. But it's political as well as social factors that have seen Chicago's blues scene, like its jazz scene, change in recent years.

'We seem to have a mayor from an Irish background who doesn't like blues,' says Bob. 'The young Mayor Daley doesn't like jazz much either and, in fact, he doesn't seem to like music bars at all. The concept seems to be that music clubs all have to be downtown and now it's harder than ever to get a liquor licence. It used to be hard to get a liquor licence before but you could always pay people off back then. Now it's just really difficult.

'It's very reminiscent of the time when the old Mayor Daley – the current Mayor Daley's father – cancelled Duke Ellington because there had been a riot at a soul music concert. Nobody would ever riot at a Duke Ellington concert – it just wasn't going to happen – but Mayor Daley didn't care. That was back in the late Sixties and early Seventies. They had to wait until Jane Byrne was mayor in Chicago in 1979 to have a jazz festival here. A few years later they had the first blues festival in the city but that wasn't until Harold Washington was mayor in the early Eighties. Now we have a white mayor, who grew up in a lily-white neighbourhood, who probably means well but is crippling local music scenes. I think he's a vast improvement on his father but it still spells trouble for music venues and taverns in the city.'

In the late Sixties and early Seventies, there were 40 or 50 clubs in the South Side of Chicago that played blues music. Theresa's was on the corner of 40th and Indiana, Pepper's was around there too, so was Florence's. Now the majority of the blues clubs are on the North Side and all that remains of the South Side blues scene is historical fact. Part of 43rd Street has been named 'Muddy Waters Boulevard' and there is a plaque up to mark this section. Muddy's house on Lake Park is also due a plaque sooner or later. But there is little more to mark the once-thriving South Side blues scene.

STILL, THERE are some that keep the fires burning on the Chicago blues scene. Koko Taylor is one of them. Koko got her first breaks sitting in on gigs in South Side bars with local artists like Muddy Waters and Howlin' Wolf. Today, she is one of the best-known blues singers in the world. But back in the 1950s, she was fresh up from the South, struggling to make ends meet like most other Southern folk who settled in the South Side of the city. Koko was just a teenager when she moved to Chicago, but already she knew Muddy and Wolf through her husband Pops who had run juke joints in West Memphis before he and Koko moved up to Chicago in the 1950s.

For the first few years after they settled in Chicago, Koko and Pops found life hard. By day Pops worked in steel mills while Koko worked as a cleaner in houses around the city. Pops was much older than Koko and had connections with musicians from his juke joint days down South and it was by night that he put these connections to use in bars and clubs around the South Side of Chicago. Pops played a bit of guitar himself but when they went to the clubs, rather than push himself forward he would say to the bands performing 'can my wife do a song?' and more often than not they would let Koko get up and perform.

It wasn't until Koko was in her thirties that blues man and Chess Records employee Willie Dixon heard her sing for the first time, while she was sitting in on a bar session with Howlin' Wolf. Dixon took her into the Chess studios the next day and produced some songs with her. Koko went on to have a few radio hits before her big hit 'Wang Dang Doodle', which was penned by Dixon and originally recorded by Howlin' Wolf in 1960. It sold over a million copies when it was released in 1966.

Koko got into the blues as a youngster, listening to artists like BB King and Big Mamma Thornton on the radio. As a teenager, it was artists like Howlin' Wolf and Muddy Waters that touched her and later, when she sang her first words alongside those greats in the South Side taverns and clubs of Chicago, it was elements of their style that she soaked up.

Koko is now 74 years old and she still plays with her band 'The Blues Machine', the very same one with whom she recorded 'Wang Dang Doodle' in 1966. Right up until the release of that record, Koko was still working as a cleaner in houses and hotels around the city. When 'Wang Dang Doodle' got to Number Four in the R&B charts in

1966, Koko started getting booked to play gigs out of town and abroad. She had some follow-up releases on Chess Records that did equally well. Then, in 1969, Leonard Chess died and Phil sold the label. Without a label, Koko's career dried up and, while she continued to perform in bars and clubs around the city, she had to return to her job as a cleaner to make ends meet. She couldn't afford to keep her band going and still worked as a maid until as late as the 1980s when her career took off again with Alligator Records.

Now, March 3rd every year marks 'Koko Taylor Day' in the city. Ask any blues fan in the city and they'll tell you that Koko remains the Queen of the Blues.

I bumped into her one day at an open-air gig in the 'Willie Dixon Blues Heaven', right next to the Chess Records Museum on the site of the old Chess studios on South Michigan. The band playing was JW Williams's band and the gig was part of the Record Row Festival. This is a series of open-air, summertime blues sessions to celebrate both Chess Records and the stretch of road on which the studio is situated, once home to a string of seminal Chicago record labels. I was sitting on the arc-shaped stone benches surrounding the miniature stage in the blues garden alongside about 20 other blues fans when Koko turned up with her daughter Cookie. The minute she walked through the gates the lead singer of the band stopped singing and announced her arrival. When they had finished the number there was a round of applause. People got up to shake Koko's hand. Others wanted their photograph taken with her. As Koko walked down the row of stone benches to take her seat at the front of the stage it seemed everybody there wanted to say hello.

Draped from the walls surrounding the open-air stage were banners of Chess Records past artists, each sporting a picture of the artist above a quotation. Etta James's said: 'I want to show that gospel, country, blues, R&B, jazz and rock'n'roll are all really just one thing.' Howlin' Wolf's read: 'These boys think they know music but they don't know life.' Muddy Waters's said: 'You gotta go to church to get this particular thing in your soul.' After the gig was over, I managed to grab a few moments with Koko to ask her what quotation she would choose for her banner, were it on display.

'Blues is a healer,' said Koko. 'That's what my banner would say. Blues music has such a meaning. Every word in a song has a meaning and that means so much to me.'

Koko still does live shows in and outside of Chicago every week. She has just released her tenth album on Alligator Records and she has no plans to stop recording and singing the blues.

'I'm going to keep on singing till I die,' she says. 'The blues is my life. I was just a teenager when I started listening to Muddy Waters and Howlin' Wolf and all of them but I just fell in love with that music as soon as I heard it. The blues spoke to me as a person. It stuck to my ribs. Muddy and Howlin' Wolf influenced me so much when I first started singing too. Muddy was a beautiful person and his singing just went through me. I just loved his singing. Every song that I would sing I would always put him in it because I loved him so much. The feeling, the meaning that goes into my music comes from Muddy. He just would always give me inspiration that I could count on. If I start writing a song I would always think about Muddy Waters. When I sing now I always think about him. Howlin' Wolf was another one that gave a lot of inspiration to me. I learnt a lot from those guys. I learned how to manoeuvre. Do things they way they did it.

'Now the blues is changing and a lot of young people have moved away from the music. People stick to what is selling and hip hop is what's selling today. Young people like hip hop 'cos they can dance off it and go crazy and these day it's the older people who are recording the blues. But I think as long as people like myself hang in there and keep singing the blues, writing it, recording it, I think maybe it will come back to where it used to be. Yeah. Somebody's got to keep the ball rolling.'

If you scour the shelves of the Jazz Record Mart you'll no doubt find some Koko Taylor releases for sale. Bob's shelves will also hold releases from contemporary blues success stories like Laurrie Bell, Johnny B Moore, Big Time Sarah and Zora Young, all of whom spend time playing and recording in the city today. Then scan the walls and you'll probably find somewhere, scotch-taped or thumb-tacked, a tatty-looking poster or dog-eared handbill. Read it carefully and it will probably tell you about a blues gig happening somewhere in the city that night or the next. If you take the next step and go to that gig then you might just experience Chicago music at its best.

6 The Gospel According To...

IT DIDN'T take long for my apartment to start resembling that murky back room of the Jazz Record Mart where I'd first caught sight of Bob Koester. Soon the vinyl and CDs I'd picked up in record stores, flea markets and thrift stores around the city seemed to be breeding. As they multiplied they began to collect in little dust-gathering clusters on every clear, flat surface in the bedroom, living room and kitchen of my apartment. Precariously balanced, irregular piles of CDs were perched on the edge of tables and chairs. On the floor and against the bedroom wall, three separate piles of vinyl had begun to stack, domino-style. Every time I accidentally brushed past the top piece, the entire stack would go cascading into the middle of the room and under the bed. But each time it happened, instead of stashing them somewhere more appropriate, I would just push the records back against the wall. Places previously reserved for sitting, eating at or preparing food on had been invaded by my growing stock until eventually my only free spot was the large spongy expanse of my bed.

Without the disapproving comments normally muttered by friends and family and untroubled by the threat of potential visitors, my new collection and I were free to live undisturbed, wallowing in our chaotic harmony. That is, until one day when I swished too eagerly past the largest stack of vinyl which I had foolishly piled by the door in my bedroom. I got my big toe caught in the round hole in the middle of the cardboard sleeve of the top piece and went crashing head first into the doorframe. Luckily wounded pride was all that I suffered. The record in question, however – a rare soul track by soul legend Curtis

Mayfield that I'd picked up for a dollar in a thrift store on Milwaukee the week before – didn't get off so lightly. I picked myself up, laid the cracked vinyl to rest, and decided to get out there and find myself a shelving unit to store my music.

The clock said 11am. It was Sunday. And that's when it hit me: I was supposed to be heading down to the 12.30pm Sunday service at Salem Baptist Church. Down in the wild hundreds on the far South Side of the city, this church, I'd been told by a reliable informant, was the church Reverend Jesse Jackson attended. In terms of music it was Salem, with its full band, choir, resident dancers and crystal-clear sound system, that was the top of the 'rock'n'roll' pile in terms of Chicago gospel churches. Chicago was the 'Gospel Capital Of The World' and so there were quite a few churches to choose from in the city – including the Fellowship Missionary Baptist Church, also on the South Side, soul star Sam Cooke's place of worship. But this one, it seemed, was the best.

I'd found out about Salem Baptist Church during a conversation I'd had with a retired pastor called Martin Deppe the week before. I didn't know he'd been a pastor at all when I'd met him for lunch downtown at the busy Rhapsody Restaurant on 35 East Adams. The reason I'd wanted to hook was because Martin, along with Sarah Pearson, my other lunch companion that day, was part of a musical organisation called the Apollo Chorus Of Chicago. The Apollo Chorus, which started in 1872, just happened to be the oldest surviving choral society in the city and the oldest, volunteer-based organisation of its kind in the whole of the United States.

I'd found out about Apollo while surfing the net for information on the Great Chicago Fire that hit the city in 1871, razing the whole of downtown Chicago to the ground soon after it had been built. I'd always remembered a song I used to sing at school that went:

> One dark night, when we were all in bed,
> Mrs O'Leary left the light on in the shed,
> The cow kicked it over, and this is what she said:
> It'll be a hot night, in the old town, tonight:
> Fire! Fire! Fire!

The song, as we used to sing it, was performed in rounds. A large group of us would be divided into smaller groups and each sub-group would sing the ditty in a staggered fashion, until the first group were singing the line 'Fire, Fire, Fire' while the last group sang the first line; and so on. The song had stuck in my mind since then but I'd had no idea, until I dug for facts on the Internet, that it referred to Chicago's Great Fire.

The fire was actually started on Sunday 8 October 1871, at around 9pm on the city's southwest side. Back then, the majority of city dwellings were built from timber harvested from the woodland areas around Lake Michigan. The week the fire struck had been a very hot spell at the end of a very hot summer. The fable has it that a local Irish lady called Mrs O'Leary had been milking her cow, and when she finished the job, she left the small oil lamp she'd been using for light burning in a corner of the hay-filled cowshed. The truth of the matter is that no one was really sure how the blaze started.

Fire tore through the city and raged on for 27 hours, killing around 250 people and destroying 17,450 buildings. Sparks from the blaze ignited forest fires that went on to destroy over a million acres of Michigan and Wisconsin timberland.

Before the fire struck, Chicago was making its mark as one of the most important cities in the United States. By the mid-1800s the city was already an established centre of commerce. The Chicago Board of Trade had been opened on 3 April 1848 by a local businessman who set up the first offices on 101 South Water Street. By 10 June that year, the first telegraphic communications between New York and Chicago had been established. Northwest University, Chicago's first, was founded in 1851 and the city's first formal police department was organised in 1855 under then Mayor Dr Levi Boone. The city had already had 13 mayors by then, after appointing its first, William B Ogden, in May 1837. Work on Chicago's Water Tower started in 1867 and by the time the Great Fire had finished rampaging through the city, this building was one of the few public buildings left standing.

From its initial incorporation on 12th August 1833 with a population of 350, the town of Chicago, by the time the Great Fire struck, had a population of 324,000. In the fire's wake, around 100,000 city residents were left homeless. These people were forced to rebuild their lives at the same time as restoring the destroyed infrastructure of the city.

As well as losing important city buildings, the impact of the Great Fire in Chicago was felt in other areas. With theatres and concert halls destroyed, the arts suffered and Chicago's plight prompted a stream of outside help. Queen Victoria and other British citizens shipped crates of books out to Chicago and, with the help of English novelist Thomas Hughes, the basis of the city's first library, the Chicago Public Library, was formed. You can still find these books in the library, not far from where I met Martin and Sarah for lunch.

The Apollo Chorus, according to their website, 'was born out of the ashes of the Great Chicago Fire by citizens who wanted to breathe cultural life back into the city'. Now with its 150 members, the chorus continues to present the greatest classical and sacred masters. Both Martin and Sarah sing in the chorus, Sarah as an alto and Martin as soprano. In addition to singing they take on the roles of Public Relations Officer and President respectively. It's the same with nearly every other member of the chorus, they told me. Everyone has their own job to hold down but, as and where they can, they devote time to the upkeep of the chorus. Sarah is a freelance writer, Martin a retired pastor. All the 150 members of the chorus, Sarah and Martin told me, meet up once a week, in between the months of September and May every year, to practise the four or five shows they put on during this period.

The chorus has been run this way since it started. Back then, said Sarah, it was an all-male group made up of very 'well-to-do and influential' members of the city. It took them a couple of years to work out that they needed women in the group and now, she told me, there are actually more women than men in the chorus.

At its height, in the first half of the 20th century, the Apollo Chorus had around 500 members. Shows around the city were performed alongside appearances at the World's Fairs. In the 1933 World's Fair, held on Chicago's Lakeshore, Martin's two aunts were both singing in the Apollo Chorus.

Now the chorus's regular shows include their annual performances of Handel's *Messiah*, for which the outfit employs the city's Baroque Orchestra. The Apollo Chorus's version of *Messiah* has been traditionally performed at the Orchestra Hall, the home of the Chicago Symphony Orchestra (CSO) that's adjoined to the Rhapsody Restaurant where we met that day. It was during that same lunch that Martin and Sarah told me that, after over a hundred years in existence, the Apollo Chorus is in the process of changing.

Attendance to classical music concerts in the city has been down in recent years. Ever since the 9/11 disaster, the arts community in the city, and indeed across the world, has suffered in line with the rest of commerce. In Chicago, this financial downturn has been the main reason that the city's CSO has been in deficit for the past few years. Chicago is lucky, Sarah told me. In other US cities the resident orchestras have been under threat of dissolution because of 9/11 and the economic downturn that's ensued. Many arts organisations in the city and around the world rely heavily on corporate sponsorship and the downturn, said Sarah, has meant that money usually donated to the arts by these huge corporations has been held back in the past couple of years. San Jose's Symphony Orchestra had to close down in 2003 as a result of these cuts; and Philadelphia's orchestra is on the brink of a similar fate.

But it's not just the blow of corporate cutbacks that has threatened the arts world. In general, said Sarah, people are going out less. There's less money around. Unemployment is high in Chicago, like in many other US cities, and money that people would have spent on going to see live classical concerts is being saved. For the Apollo Chorus, which since its inception has survived solely on ticket sales, this is bad news. As a result the organisation is trying to change its format. The only way out of this situation is to try to reel in a new audience to supplement the dwindling crowd.

It's not just the Apollo Chorus that is having to adapt to the times either. Other arts events organisations are having to rethink their programmes in order to win the audiences in this time of declining ticket sales. The Ravinia Festival, a summer-long, outdoor classical music event held every year in Hyland Park, in a northern suburb of Chicago, has been incorporating jazz and pop music into its line-up to attract more people. The Apollo Chorus performed at the last Ravinia Festival. In the future though, Martin told me, things are going to have to change.

'We're in a transitional time, I would say,' he said in the restaurant that afternoon. 'Music has diversified so much and technology has allowed people to bring music into their homes. The high quality of CDs just means that people can now, in a sense, create their own program at home. That has taken away some attendance. Also the younger people are looking for a broader range of music. So really the traditional audience is dwindling as the population is getting older. We are now in the process of trying to reflect these changes and deal with them as a challenge. And do the kind of music that is both inspiring to us as singers and will really reach an audience of the 21st century.'

One of the problems Martin sees with the city's classical music scene is the fact that people don't have much chance to hear classical pieces on the radio. With only one, privately run, classical station in Chicago, there is no other outlet through which people can hear classical pieces, unless they go and hear them live. But it isn't just the lack of exposure to classical music on the radio that's the problem.

'There's not much diversity on the radio,' said Martin. 'They play all the great masterpieces and they don't play a lot of the wonderful music that surrounds that. To me all Bach's music is great; but Mozart wrote some stuff that, while it's not at the same level and it's not played, is still great music. It's still Mozart. There are other symphonies besides Beethoven's Fifth and Brückner's Seventh. There's a lot that they don't touch on the station that we'd love to hear.'

It's those elements of classical music, the ones left out of the mainstream, that Martin and Sarah also want to weave into the Chorus's repertoire. In 1997, the chorus appointed a new musical director/conductor Dr Stephan Alltop. Now they are thinking of appointing a General Manager too. With no official office and only one dusty storeroom in the Fine Arts building just a short walk from the Rhapsody on North Michigan Avenue – they practise here each week looking out on the brilliant Navy Pier opposite – both Martin and Sarah think that it might be time for the Apollo Chorus to move into the 21st century. It's no less than 152 years since the Great Fire of Chicago and 151 years since the Apollo Chorus started – and so perhaps change is well overdue.

MARTIN DEPPE is 64 years old. Measuring in somewhere around the six-foot mark with broad shoulders and a kind but striking face it's not hard to imagine him whipping up a frenzy at the pulpit. His grey hair is cut long to suit his long, thin face; and this face eases into a smile that, judging by the laughter lines around his eyes, he's been familiar with for a good many years. Martin retired two years ago. In his 39 years as a preacher, he had six churches in and around Chicago. One of those was the First Methodist Church at Evanston, Illinois, which hosted the 1954 second session of the World Council of Churches.

After Evanston Martin had a church in a South Side Chicago area called Gresham, further south from the troubled Englewood area. Martin was pastor of this church at a time when Chicago real estate people were turning over the city's neighbourhoods in a controversial process called red-lining. According to Martin, real estate managers took a map of Chicago and marked in red the communities and streets they were giving up. Then they'd scare the whites that lived there into fleeing and charge twice as much for blacks to buy. Martin was pastor of the church in Gresham just as this was happening in the area.

'At one point I had an all-white worshipping congregation at 11am after an all-black Sunday school at 9 o'clock,' remembered Martin. 'The black parents were testing the church with their kids. I learned a lot about the black American heritage in that church. I learned a lot about myself too and about people in general: the freedom of the body for example; the ability to let the whole body express itself. I don't mean just in a complete frenzy – but I mean in a more emotional way. This was reflected in a more emotional style of singing. It's not just about the voice – it's about the whole body. You need to breathe both through your entire diaphragm, which is your back, as well as your front. With great singers you see their back move as they sing. Your back expands so that the whole diaphragm is used. The first time I experienced this kind of singing was in my church in Gresham.'

Being pastor in the black community led to Martin having a strong involvement in the Civil Rights movement of the 1950s and 1960s. It was during this time that he worked for an outfit designed to improve economic conditions in the black community and bring about social change. Although Martin worked with Civil Rights activists Jesse Jackson and Martin Luther King in Operation Breadbasket, he tells me that his enrolment into the organisation came quite by chance.

'I was in the black church one day and my bishop said to me, "well, can you go to this meeting for me". 'He should have sent a black pastor but he sent me and I got involved. I ended up hiring Jesse Jackson from King's staff to run Operation Breadbasket, which was an economic arm of the Civil Rights Movement in which we used the power of the black pulpit. In the black community the pulpit is the major force. The church is where the leadership emerged, because it was their church. It wasn't the white man's church. So the black leadership came through the black church. They could use the power of the pulpit to say "hey, Coca Cola is using white drivers in the community, they're making money out of the black community, we need to see them use some black people in their business". It was a very legitimate demand and we made a lot of progress in those years.

'King brought that operation to Chicago. We hired Jesse. We went from corporation to corporation and just laid out the statistics. "You are in Chicago, we have 20% black people in the city and you have 1% in your workforce and they're all at the bottom." So we would negotiate with them and if they started giving us trouble, we went to the pulpits and said "don't buy Coca Cola". I'm telling you, we got a helluva quick reaction. It was a good project.

'Operation Breadbasket united the black churches. We met every Friday afternoon in one of the black churches and we had this strong organisation. It was mostly black pastors. I was just a freak. I was one of the three or four whites that were in that organisation. But they treated us totally equally. Colour was not in the picture in that operation. I'm still a close friend of Jesse although I get mad at him all the time. I'm certain he goes to Salem Baptist Church because the pastor at Salem was his Executive Director with Operation PUSH (People United To Serve Humanity) for a long time. Jackson developed Operation PUSH in the late Sixties and early 1970s. They are close friends. That's his church.'

As Martin looked through the pages of his small, black notebook for the exact address of Salem Baptist Church, I examined the dwindling lunchtime crowd at the Rhapsody. A few people were left in the smart, main dining hall, sipping after-lunch coffee from white china cups and saucers or paying their bills and heading out into the sunshine. It was while watching one particular couple paying their bill that I noticed someone standing right by me at our table. I looked up and a large, black lady dressed in a smart green dress with dark, tight-curled, shoulder-length hair, a good dose of chocolate-brown freckles scattered across her cheeks and nose and the warmest, widest grin in the room was standing opposite Martin smiling.

'This is such a small world,' she said, widening her grin and extending her hand to Martin, who looked up, slightly confused, from his notebook. 'I just wanted to shake your hand. I was just sitting here thinking I should go back to work but I couldn't help overhearing your conversation. I was trying not to mind your business but then I heard you talking about Operation Breadbasket and I thought to myself, I bet you I was right shoulder to shoulder with him. I looked totally different then. I was a skinny little thing. But I was one of the Freedom Singers in the Rainbow PUSH choir in the Sixties. I rode on the bus as a teenager. We'd sing at the different rallies. I attended school in North Carolina where Reverend Jackson used to be. My father was a history professor and worked in North Carolina. My mom was from Chicago. They were divorced. My father was a history professor and very active in the movement too. He had me involved. My mother couldn't stand it. She thought it was dangerous. I was a teenager and I could sing first soprano and I used to travel with them as a Freedom Singer all over the country.'

This friendly woman was called Jacqueline Eaton. As she told her story that afternoon, Martin stared at her open-mouthed, shaking his head and uttering the words 'for God's sakes' every now and then. As they talked, I remembered something avant garde jazz player Ken Vandermark had said to me weeks before about how Chicago was 'a big city with a small-town attitude'. As I listened to Martin and Jacqueline swap stories of troubled, exciting times before I was even born, I couldn't help but feel a strange sense of comfort. I might be here, in the company of strangers, all on my own in a big, unfamiliar city but in fact this city was just part of a very small world.

'Did you know Ben Branch?' Martin asked Jacqueline, as I tuned back into their conversation. 'He directed our orchestra,' Martin continued.

'Yes I absolutely do know him,' said Jacqueline.

'When King was killed he was talking to Ben. They were in the parking lot of the Lorraine Motel where Dr King was shot. King was talking to Ben and he said to Ben "I want you to do 'Amazing Grace' tonight". Then he was shot right at that moment. But he was our band director. Ben Branch. Yes he was.'

'Well you know this is such a small world,' said Jacqueline. She turned to me.

'Reverend Meeks's church, Salem, is on Indiana. East of State and at Indiana, right on the corner of 118th Street,' she said. 'You got to go to the 12.30pm service but you got to go early because it's crowded. Just go there and ask for my friend Charlotte Timms. I'll call her and leave a message that you're coming.'

IT WAS chaos outside Salem Church as my taxi pulled up as close as we could get to the door. In the wet gloom I could just make out the entrance of Salem, a big, warm rectangle of light at the top of a short flight of stairs. Rain thundered out of the sky. Hot wind whipped the drops in every direction as cars, mini-buses, vans, coaches and people on foot struggled to get to the front doors of the large, grey-stone building sitting on the corner of 118th and Indiana. I opened the taxi door and an ankle-deep stream of water gushed just below my feet and I wondered how I would make it from the taxi to the front door of the church without getting soaked.

Families in their Sunday best struggled under umbrellas, picking a path to the door of the church. Children ran from packed cars to the shelter of the doorway and all the while the black sky thundered and bellowed, spewing out its hot, wet drops onto the Salem congregation. I paid the taxi driver the $30 cab fare – an expensive ride by Chicago standards – and made my dash for it.

Inside the church the combination of lilac-painted walls, high ceilings and all-engulfing swell of music channelled via an intricate speaker system hooked up to the band at the front of the church engulfed me like a bear hug. Many people were already in their seats, others were being ushered there by men and women who seemed to be wearing some sort of uniform. The church was vast – bigger than a standard basketball court with ceiling so high I had to throw my head right back to see the top of the roof. I approached one of the ushers, all wearing pastel-green suits, and asked for Charlotte Timms.

'She's out back somewhere getting ready,' the usher said, before guiding me right to the front of the church, on the right-hand wing of two rows of long, thick wooden benches. The front row was made up of fold-away seats and I was put into the middle seat in the row and told that I would be able to speak to Charlotte after the service. From this spot, I had full view of the stage just in front of me, while behind me the rows and rows of seats were slowly filling. It was 12.15pm, just fifteen minutes before the service was due to start.

Right in front of me in a cordoned-off section of the stage was the band and already they were playing. Led by the piano the gentle, soulful music was amplified and pumped out across the church via a string of speakers attached to the walls on either side of the building. The choir was in place. All dressed in the same pastel green as the ushers, the collection of men and women were formed in a large semi-circle in the centre of the stage. In the middle of the arc made by the choir was a tall, clear-glass, gilt-edged pulpit.

Behind the pulpit and the choir and positioned below a large, white-framed, stained-glass window was a large, rectangular screen. Around the church, four or five men with television cameras were filming the congregation coming in and sitting down and it was these images that were being projected onto the screen. As the women, men and children filed into their seats and took their places, I watched the whole thing on the screen in front of me. People of all ages came alone, with their families, with friends or in couples and within minutes every seat in the church was full. On the screen I got a view of the entire church, a sea of happy, excited faces and even my own, standing out of the crowd of at least 1,000 people as the only white face there.

As the service progressed I got to see, first-hand, a little bit about what Martin Deppe had described as the 'emotional expression' he learned all those years ago in his church in Gresham. In response to Reverend James Meeks's sermon, the gusto of shouts like 'Oh come on, Reverend!', 'Yes, Yes!' and 'Preach It! Preach it!' were rivalled only by the energy of the congregation in song. Most of the songs were uplifting, soulful, piano-led tunes that I couldn't recognise. Each time the band played another song the congregation would clap, shout and sing. Dancers in colourful robes – a group called the Fellowship Of David, as I later discovered – danced in and out of the aisles in the church. The choir led the crowd in song and all the while a woman at the front of the stage translated the words and lyrics into sign language. I was shocked halfway through one of the songs to see myself on the screen, dancing and clapping right along with everyone else in the congregation.

After the service I managed to find Charlotte Timms. She was one of the choir who'd been at the front of the crowd the entire way through the service, and she explained to me the way things work at Salem.

'The 12.30pm crowd at Salem really get to be off the hook,' she said. 'We have a 7.30am, 10am and 12.30pm service on Sundays. The 7.30am crowd are more subdued because it's early. It's generally older people that come to that. They want to come to church, get into the song and clap but they won't get into it too much because they want to sit down and hear what the pastor has to say. They're more the seasoned saints. 10am are an upbeat crazy kind of crowd. They get a chance to let loose more than the other crowds do and the 12.30pm crowd are getting that way too.'

Charlotte is just one of the full-time employees of Salem, a church that started in this neighbourhood back in 1985 with a congregation of just 250. Since then, its congregation has steadily grown and soon it will begin on the construction of a new church, just near this one on 118th South Indiana, so that they can fit all the people in that want to come. She has been singing in church since she was a child and over the years has seen the music change.

'Music soothes that thing in you,' says Charlotte. 'I always say that people come to church with a lot of different baggage. Problems. So when people come to church, they need something to sort of calm them down. Something to help them forget about what it is they are going through. When you start off with praise, worship and music – it sort of helps them to forget and it also prepares them for the pastor. When the pastor comes up to speak he shouldn't have to work so hard. He doesn't have to work so hard in his sermon because the people are already calm and wanting more. Music is very important.

'The music we play and sing in the church is very different to music you get outside of church. Secular music appeases materialistic things. Church music appeases spiritual things. Look at the blues. The blues is poetry that soothes but it's still feeding the body, it's not feeding your spirit. It's not going to last. In a minute you're going to forget about it. When you relate to lyrics like "my baby left me" you're not feeding your spirit because you're talking about materialistic things. You're talking about another body. A person. With your spirit it's feeding your inner man and that's what's gonna help your outer man – that's what the sermon today was all about.'

The person in charge of music at Salem Church is a large, merry-looking, 34-year-old man called Terry Moore and it's he who composed all the music for the service that's just ended. He's been programming the music at Salem for the past six years and, in that time, has collated the best gospel band of any church in the whole of Chicago. Outside of his work with Salem he's worked with some of the most prominent gospel artists in the city. Gospel stars like Yolanda Adams, Andrae Crouch, Walter Hawkins and Daryl Coley all have records out featuring Terry – on gospel labels like Word Records and Savoy.

At Salem Terry leads the band with the piano, but he can play any instrument out there. Piano, drums, bass guitar, percussion, guitar, lead guitar, organ and synths make up the Salem band – and Terry is adept on all of them. His story, he tells me, is fairly traditional in the context of many of the gospel musicians in Chicago.

'I was seven when I started playing,' he says. 'I've been playing in church all my life. I actually started on bass guitar. My parents bought me this cheap bass guitar at the time. Then I shifted from bass guitar to piano. I've been playing piano since then. A lot of American music and a lot of black American music has a gospel flavour to it. Especially this new neo-soul kind of thing: There's a big gospel flavour to all of that stuff.

'Chicago is the gospel mecca but to be honest, a lot of the secular artists come to the church to get their lead singers, their background singers and their musicians. People like Anastasia, Beyoncé, Backstreet Boys, Aretha Franklin, Earth, Wind & Fire and Patti La Belle – all those people have used musicians right here from Chicago. I got to work with Stevie Wonder in that way. Stevie knew someone I'd worked with and said he needed someone so I ended up playing with Stevie Wonder on the Oprah Winfrey Show. That was early last year.

'I actually do all the arrangements for all of the music here. I serve as the executive music director so I've pulled the band in too. Our guitar player here used to work with Luther Vandross. The percussionist has played for Barry Manilow. The good thing about our band is that they come from everywhere so we have, in a sense, got the best we can get. Outside of Salem though, I still get time to arrange music for some of the best gospel band players in the business.

'Most of the music I compose is worked out of my prayer life with God or from reading the word of God. So a lot of the arrangements that God gives me come out of that. Usually I'm in prayer or I'm reading the Word and that's when it all comes. A lot of it is during service, there's a lot of spontaneous stuff too. Usually we work with contemporary-sounding music here but from time to time we work on updated versions of what we call in the black church traditional music or hymns. Stuff like "Amazing Grace" that was composed by Thomas Dorsey – that's traditional music.'

Dorsey, known as 'The Father Of Gospel Music', coined the term 'gospel songs' in the 1920s. It was a term he used for religious songs that had the bounce and pep of early jazz and blues music and it was this style of song that he later devoted a big part of his life to creating. His first non-secular composition was 'Precious Lord, Take My Hand', written just days after the death of his wife and child in 1932. By the end of that year, Dorsey had put together the Theodore Roosevelt Frye gospel choir – the first ever gospel choir in the US – at Ebenezer Baptist Church in Chicago. The following year the first-ever National Convention of Gospel Choirs and Choruses was held in the city at the Pilgrim Baptist Church. It was this convention that ushered in the golden age of gospel.

With a strong beat and full chords, gospel piano playing drew on the influences of Chicago-based ragtime jazz players like Scott Joplin and WC Handy – both of whom had a history of playing in church. Church groups, focusing on strong vocals, started forming in the city and it wasn't long before Chicago had bred its first gospel star Mahalia Jackson. Jackson moved to Chicago at age 15, started singing in church, and by the time she was 22 she had become a well-known local singer. Her powerful voice lent well to the emotive-style gospel music and when Dorsey heard her sing, he found a muse. They began working together in the late 1930s and penned a string of gospel hits during that time.

'All the gospel music you hear today is based on what Thomas Dorsey started,' says Terry. 'There are lots of different styles of church music and down the years people have taken their own version of whatever and branched out and now everyone has their own style.'

Today's contemporary gospel music is filled with uplifting lyrics, mellifluous melodies and complex rhythm fills. It's this use of distinctive rhythms and syncopations that can be traced back to African music traditions. So too can the 'call and response' singing style in gospel and spiritual music – a style of singing where one vocalist sings a phrase that is repeated, or answered, by another vocalist or a group of singers.

When slaves came from Africa to America in the 1800s they brought their music with them. Forbidden from using drums by their masters, slaves would sing work songs while they were working – with lyrics that focused on oppression, hardship and ill-treatment – and later on in church these same songs leant themselves to the themes featured in the Bible. The themes of the work songs translated well in churches, where song became an important part of worship in the black community. The themes of contemporary church music, insists Charlotte, haven't changed so much since those early days.

'For a singer in church the music is still a heartfelt thing,' she says. 'It's not something that you can just do because you can just do it. It's something that you have to feel when you do it. Especially in church. You want to sing so that the people are feeling what you are singing. As a praise and worship leader – which is what we are when we sing in front like I do – it's my job to take the people out there where I am. Those people are hurting. They are hurting, so I have to make sure that I get them. It could be by an expression. It could be through the song. Whatever it is, I've got to make sure that I get through to them when I sing.'

Salem Church is just one of the churches in Chicago that uses music to get its message across. The message now, just as it was back then, is to go after a better and more spiritual life. According to Charlotte, Pastor Meeks has been integral in trying to change Roselyn from an impoverished neighbourhood into a community that nurtures its residents. 'Years ago,' says Charlotte, 'the neighbourhood had lots of businesses, companies and furniture stores. Before long all those had gone from the area to be replaced by liquor stores, corner stores, people hanging out on the corner drinking, smoking, getting high, playing cards. It's the same with a lot of areas on the South Side of the city.'

Salem Church is opening its new 'complex', three blocks from Salem on 115th Street. They're calling it the 'Multi-Purpose Center', although Charlotte says it's more of a 'stadium' than a church. It will make Roselyn 'better and bigger'. Alongside the church, there will be a sports arena, where local kids can come and play basketball and soccer, together with a new building for Salem's 'youth ministry'. According to Charlotte, a big factor in the youth ministry is music, which she describes as 'the soul of everything'. While kids all over Chicago get down to the bump 'n' grind of rap and R&B, Charlotte believes that the Youth Ministry will enable local kids to get in touch with music that will 'feed their spirit'.

By the time I left Salem that morning I felt refreshed. I'm usually fairly reserved in public places and definitely aware that my singing voice is best confined to the bathroom, and so I was amazed at how I'd spent the hour or so in Salem's congregation singing at the top of my voice, flailing my arms, dancing and clapping. Pastor Meeks's sermon about 'denying the desires of the flesh' wasn't something I was going to take to heart or home, but the music and song I'd heard had certainly left a deep impression.

When I stepped out of Salem and down onto 118th Street, the black clouds were gone from the sky and the dull, grey blanket they'd left behind was slashed with streaks of pure blue. Through those widening gashes, the sun was burning hot and bright, lighting up the puddles on the street and bringing life to the wet, glistening pavements. Charlotte had told me that midsummer storms in Chicago might be fierce, but they don't last long and as I made my way to the overground, Metra Line station on 115th and Cottage Grove I had a feeling there would be no more rain that day.

The heart of Chicago: the El train shooting through the Loop.

King of the Blues:
the late, great
Muddy Waters
strums his guitar.

Outside Fred Anderson's Velvet Lounge on the near South Side.

Fred Anderson practises before opening time at the Velvet Lounge.

Buddy Guy, Chicago's greatest living blues legend.

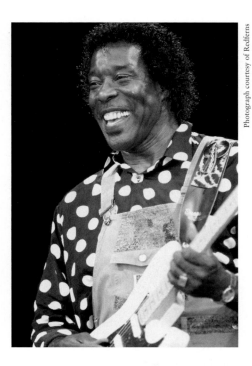

Outside Chess Records studios, on the famed Record Row.

Bruce Iglauer in his office at
Alligator Records.

Nan Warshaw, co-founder of
Bloodshot Records, at her office.

Jazz in the Wild
Hundreds: the New
Apartment Lounge.

Von Freeman at his Tuesday night jam session at the New Apartment Lounge.

Outside the HotHouse just before Yoko Noge's Monday night session.

Frankie Knuckles:
The Godfather of
house music.

House producer Cajmere
(aka Curtis Jones) at his
Cajual/Relief offices.

Photograph courtesy of Redferns

Steve Albini, legendary producer and musician – without his overalls.

Afternoon browsing at the Jazz Record Mart.

Koko Taylor at Willie Dixon's
Blues Heaven Garden.

Lil' Ed performs with his Blues
Imperial Band on a hot
Saturday night at B.L.U.E.S on
Halstead.

7 Rock Starts Rolling

STILL stinging from the cracked Mayfield record, I was determined to get my newly acquired vinyl and CD collection organised. I'd bought a secondhand pine shelving unit for $108 from a local thrift store. It was a snip at the price, especially considering that the five-shelf-high stack was deep enough to accommodate a 12" vinyl piece and that the treated wood, despite being shot through with ancient woodworm tunnels, was strong enough to hold my growing stash.

The fun part was arranging the records and CDs on the shelves. The vinyl – I'd accumulated about 90 pieces by now – was to take up the bottom three shelves while CDs were allotted the top two. Armed with a six-pack of beer, a large bag of spicy, smoked bar-b-que chips and soothed by the mellow drone of Fenton Robinson's voice on his *Somebody Load Me A Dime* album (his brilliant 1974-released debut for Alligator Records), I set about my task one sunny Saturday afternoon.

I'd put the shelf against the wall in the living room. From here it was just near enough to the window to make the most of the light cutting through the horizontal blinds in clean, clear slices, but far enough away from the hot, thin rays not to risk any damage to the vinyl. Sitting cross-legged on the floor, I began my task, determined to start from the bottom shelf – left-hand side first of course – and make my way gradually to the very top. I picked up the first piece of vinyl: Quincy Jones' *I'll Be Good To You*. It was the 1989 'Around The House Mix' of the soul-funk classic, including the original version with

Ray Charles and Chaka Khan that I'd found, and looking at it made me smile. Jones famously produced Michael Jackson's 1982-released *Thriller* album but it was always his pop-soul singles that I loved best and this was just another to add to my collection.

I dusted the sleeve down with a t-shirt and put it on the shelf. It slipped down onto its back and so I propped it up again with one hand and took a handful of chips with the other, shoving the lot into my mouth. Reaching over to grab a loose CD, I put this in place to hold up the vinyl so it wouldn't slip again and, taking a large slug of my cold beer to wash down the spicy, salty chips, I picked up the next piece of vinyl. It was a battered original LP version of Big Black's *Songs About Fucking*. The track list on the back of the sleeve transported me back nearly 15 years and, smiling, I threw my head back and chanted the lyrics to 'Kerosene', drowning out Fenton with my yells. How could I put a Big Black LP snugly up against a Quincy Jones 12"? The two couldn't be more different. Okay, Quincy Jones and Big Black guitarist Steve Albini are both important modern music producers of the latter half of 20th century, but to place them sleeve-to-sleeve on a pine shelving unit just felt wrong. If I continued thus, randomly placing rock against soul, house against jazz, how would I find anything again when I was next looking in a hurry? It would be impossible.

I picked up the next flat slab of vinyl – a double-pack original LP version of Mayfield's 1972-released, soul-funk masterpiece *Superfly*. Gazing at its cover, I grinned the smile of the triumphant – how lucky I was to have found a copy of that lurking in the bins of Reckless Records! I definitely was positioned in one of the best neighbourhoods in the city for record shopping. But my smile faded fast when the breadth of my plight hit me again. Staring at the pile of records and CDs that surrounded me on the wooden floor of my apartment just as Fenton crooned the opening lines to 'King Of Fools', I realised I would have to rethink my assignment. I should have known better really. I'd sweated sweet, agonising hours back at home deciding how to store my vinyl and CD collection. Was it best to divide the whole lot by genre, or alphabetically by artist? Once I'd decided on the main category divisions, how best was it to split those? Chronologically or alphabetically by title? It was a big problem whichever way you looked at it. Eventually I'd decided my home collection was best split by genre, then chronologically. I had around 4,000 records and at least 2,000 CDs at home, so it had been an important decision to make. Since I'd made it, I was still unconvinced that I'd opted for the best arrangement and often found myself scouring my shelves at home for far too long, desperately searching for a particular piece.

Now, in a new city with a new collection that was growing by the day, I was faced with the same dilemma again. But surely with such a small collection it would be easy to divide the whole lot chronologically with separate time lines for CDs and vinyl? And was it really worth splitting singles and albums in the vinyl section when there were only 90 pieces in total so far? But applying the chronological system to the whole lot would mean remembering exactly when a single or album had been pressed – and on a fuzzy Sunday morning or a booze-bleary Saturday night that wasn't always the easiest task. It would be far easier, I decided, to separate the sections by genre. Jazz, blues, soul, punk, R&B, hip hop, house and 'other'. Easy.

But then I remembered, this was Chicago music I was dealing with. All the records and CDs in my small collection were by Chicago artists – spanning nearly a century of music written and recorded in the city. While some of the artists were easily classifiable by genre, others were sonic chameleons who, over their years making music, had ducked in and out of styles. Etta James? A blues singer or a soul star? Herbie Hancock? A jazz pianist or R&B legend? R Kelly? An R&B star or an out-and-out popster? It wasn't so easy to say either one or the other. If I didn't get it right from the start I could face weeks of confusion, unable to find the exact record or CD I was looking for at the exact time that I needed it.

Frustration loomed. Removing the two pieces of vinyl I'd already placed on the shelf and putting them back on the original pile, I paused for a moment. With my hand on top of the stack I decided to unsettle the lot, smoothing the pile out flat until the entire space on my living room floor was covered in single pieces of vinyl. Kneeling at one end of the room, I could see all 90 pieces fanning out as far as the hall leading to the kitchen. I stared at the sea of familiar faces gazing back at me from picture sleeves, sitting amid a sea of blank, hole-punched sleeves similar to the one that had caught my big toe the other day. It was a rare Chess Records 12" that my eyes eventually settled on. It was one of the label's early releases, cut soon after its owners had closed down its predecessor imprint Aristocrat – also based in the city – and re-started under the new name, Chess. I picked out the piece, comfortingly older than me according to the date printed on it, dusted it down and took another slug of beer.

I'd read a lot about Chess Records before coming to the city and since I'd been here I'd seen and heard a lot of its legacy around, in the bars and clubs of the metropolis. I'd read about how tours of the former studio site – now known as the Willie Dixon Blues Heaven Foundation – happen on a daily basis. Chess Records' Leonard and Phil Chess ran the label at the site on Michigan Avenue from 1957 to 1967. The building was later bought by Chess employee Willie Dixon's wife, Marie Dixon, and she in turn donated it to the Blues Heaven Foundation, an organisation that Willie had started in an effort to keep the blues tradition in Chicago alive. Willie died in 1992 but the site has remained open to the public. This was etched in my brain as one of the 'definites' on my mental 'things to do in Chicago' list. Unable to find pictures of the studios in books, magazines or on the web I'd naturally resorted to fantasy for my picture-painting of what I would find when I finally made it to 2120 South Michigan Avenue.

That address is also the name of a Rolling Stones song and the band famously made a pilgrimage to Chicago in 1964 to get to the heart of where the music that had such a huge influence on their sound had been made. It was Muddy's slide guitar antics, alongside the sexually driven, angst-ridden themes in his lyrics, on which the Stones based a large part of their style. Muddy had picked up slide guitar from Delta blues star Son House. Back then Son would use a bottleneck that he'd place on his middle finger and run up and down the string above a fret, hence the name 'bottlenecking' that is used to refer to slide guitar. With the other hand he would pick at that same string, resulting in a sound that was rhythmic yet distorted and that lent well to the mood of blues music. Nowadays, small metal tubes are used instead of bottlenecks, but the effect is the same.

Son was a huge influence on Muddy. When Muddy moved to Chicago in the 1940s, he put a modern twist on the slide guitar sound by playing in on the electric guitar, which added depth to the distortion of the notes.

Muddy Waters was a sex symbol of his time, performing to crowds of screaming female fans years before Elvis Presley made an art out of doing his snakey-hipped thing. With his crooned lyrics and smouldering eyes, Muddy generated hysteria whenever he performed and his well-known love of the ladies wasn't held back when it came to getting to know female fans individually after his gigs. Muddy was one of the first artists of the 20th century to discover that innate, indefinable 'thing' that later became known as star quality. He was one of the first singers to become an idol, a theme that lies at the heart of pop stardom and rock'n'roll music today. Men wanted to be him and women just wanted him. Stories about Muddy's penchant for the ladies were well known at the time and this part of the blues man's legend lives on.

Alligator Records' owner Bruce Iglauer, when I'd met him in his office that afternoon, described the one and only 'black gig' he saw Muddy play. The date was New Year's Eve, 1962. The place was a club called The White Rose, in Phoenix, Illinois; an unincorporated suburb of Chicago controlled only by the County Sheriff. The White Rose, remembered Bruce, was the most 'wide open' blues club he ever saw in his life.

'There was gambling,' Bruce remembered. 'There was prostitution. The concept of "closing time" was not in their vocabulary. I saw Muddy play but that night he wasn't "Muddy Waters the Godfather of the blues". I saw "Muddy Waters the man who fucked his way across the South Side and never left a customer unsatisfied". That was his reputation.

'That night I saw Muddy with all these women, many of whom he had probably slept with, or who wanted to sleep with him. Muddy had

had an auto accident – he was on crutches – but as far as these women were concerned this was the sexiest man they'd ever seen. He had those bedroom eyes. And that voice! I'm not a big fan of big, hefty women but I know a lot of black guys who are; and Muddy certainly was. He was surrounded by women that night, some of them who were about 300 pounds in weight; and he seemed to be keeping all of them happy. The reason that they wanted to be with him was that he walked in and the neon sign flashing above his head said "I am the most self-confident man you have ever seen in your life. I am so sure of myself that you would just die to be me". There was just so much presence from him as a human being.'

Anyone I asked in the city who knew Muddy, or had seen him perform, agreed that sexuality was as much an ingredient of his performance as his slide guitar prowess and his inimitable vocals. Muddy's guitar playing was something that Stones frontman Mick Jagger has oft cited as one of his main influences but it was Muddy's stage presence, and his overt sexuality when performing, that Jagger also adopted. It's a potency that Jagger quite clearly tapped into and put directly into practice during his career.

When the Stones turned up at the Chess Studios for their recording session, legend has it that they found Muddy painting the basement of the building. Muddy, like many artists on the Chess roster at the time, was successful but broke and doing odd jobs to earn some cash to tide him over while he waited for his royalty cheque to come through. Muddy wasn't the only Chess artist to be employed by the label outside of a musical capacity. The wonderful Minnie Ripperton worked on reception at the studios after graduating high school and was soon releasing her first cuts for the label in the Sixties as the singer with all-girl group The Gems. After that group split, Ripperton went on to record solo for the label releasing a single 'Lonely Girl' under the name Andrea Davis. Singing with psychedelic soul band Rotary Connection, Ripperton later featured on the release of that band's eponymous album in 1968 on Chess Records offshoot label Cadet.

In my fantasy-image of the studios as they are today, I had hoped that my ten dollars – that's the cost for the guided tour – would take me on a tour of a place preserved since those times. I pictured myself wandering around the dusty studios, the drone of the tour guide bubbling in the background, while I was transported back to times when Chuck Berry slept on a shabby cot in the drab basement of the building. The label was too tight to put him up in a city hotel. Chess was notorious for underpaying its artists and for taking far too long to deliver their royalty cheques.

The reality, when I arrived at the studios, was disappointing. From outside the glass-fronted site, where the offices once stood, had clearly been recently renovated and was more tailored to the tourist crowds than designed to retain any authenticity. The 20-minute tours of the Chess Studios, I'd read before arriving in the city, happen weekdays from 9.30am to 5.30pm. The idea is that you phone beforehand to check if the tours are running, turn up, pay your ten dollars and take the tour. I'd phoned ahead and was told by the friendly person manning the phone to 'just turn up' at the site between 9.30am and 5pm. When I turned up as directed, the studio was closed. The doorbell outside the building threw up no answer and the phone number, when I rang it to check what was going on, merely went through to ansaphone. After seeing the outside of the studio and reading the description of the tour on the poster stuck to the inside of the glass front I decided against it anyway, resolving to return the following week to the open-air festival.

While I was in the area I decided to check out the immediate surroundings. If the Chess building, just south of the Loop, was fairly nondescript, then the buildings around it were equally unexciting to the untrained eye. The Willie Dixon Blues Heaven Foundation might stand slap in the middle of the 12-block area of South Michigan Avenue, stretching from 12th Street to 24th Street and known as Chicago's 'Record Row' or 'Music Mile', but you certainly wouldn't know it by walking past it. There is a road sign that labels this section of South Michigan 'Record Row' – but blink and you'd miss it. The whole thing seemed strange to me, especially considering the fact that between 1950 and 1980 this stretch of road was home to a string of independent recording companies including Chess, Chance, Vee Jay, King and Brunswick. Taken as a group those imprints were responsible for releasing some of the most important early blues, R&B and soul music ever made. Also housed on record row during that period was the famous All State Distributing Company that had 36 labels on its books, including Chess and out-of-town imprints Checker, Motown, Stax and Smash.

Now there's little sign of what went on here during the 1950s and 1960s. Those two decades marked a time in the city when music styles were shifting and changing and most of those changes were initiated here in this nondescript, uncelebrated part of the city.

By the 1950s, Chicago's jazz-infused, recently formed jump-up blues sound was adopting new themes and going from being a black, urban sound to a more widespread phenomenon. The Chicago blues sound lent itself well to the lyrics and themes in the songs that were becoming popular. Artists like Muddy Waters, Howlin' Wolf, Little Walter and Bo Diddley all contributed to this new, energetic take on the blues – not simply with their distinctive musical styles, but also with their performance techniques and connection of music, performance and persona in a distinguishable manner that would go on to be one of the main characteristics of rock'n'roll music.

The music produced and released by labels like Chess, Vee Jay and Chance drew from a pool of largely black musicians and artists. Other labels resorted to offshoot, smaller imprints to release these 'race records', as they were called at the time. But here in Chicago, Chess and the other labels on Record Row devoted their entire catalogue to this niche music and ushered in the R&B era through these releases.

Apart from Vee Jay – which was started in 1953 by husband and wife duo Jimmy Bracken and Vivien Carter – the labels on Record Row were all run by white folk. The black musicians on these labels' rosters were, in general, badly paid for their art but the music scene in the 1950s and 1960s was nonetheless changing for the better and moving in favour of the artist.

In 1949 a *Billboard* magazine reporter named Jerry Wexler – he later went on to become head of Atlantic Records – created the term 'R&B' as another way of describing 'race records', which was the term then used for music made by black artists and released on white-owned labels. Bluebird beat – the term that referred to the black Chicago blues music released in the late 1930s – came directly from the Bluebird Records label, a 'race label' that was launched as an offshoot of Victor to release black music. R&B referred directly to the words 'rhythm and blues' but what the term really meant was 'black American popular music', particularly records made in the period after World War Two. Characteristic of R&B was a combination of blues, jazz and gospel themes. By the mid-Fifties, R&B was breaking through ethnic barriers and gaining increased visibility in the white popular music scene. Black music had done that previously but it was during this period that the music began to sell fast and attract attention outside of the States and across Europe.

Ask someone like Bob Koester, who will assert that 'some of his best friends are white', and he'll tell you that 'the music would have been important even if no British rock people had ever gotten interested in it'. But of course, he maintains, once the British got interested in it, the Americans paid a little more respect to it and started listening to it a bit more. This, in turn, injected a new sense of pride and vigour into urban black culture in America.

Listen to songs like the Willie Dixon-penned 'Hoochie Coochie Man', recorded by Muddy Waters for Chess in 1954, and Bo Diddley's 'I'm A Man', recorded for the label in 1955, and you'll hear the message that the black man's patience at being badly treated was coming to an end.

This new burst of masculinity and vigour in the music wasn't just about getting across a social message either. The emotionally intense lyrics in R&B music often referred both blatantly and inadvertently to sex, dancing and the 'I can't be satisfied' ethos that lay at the heart of what we now call teenage angst. The music itself was charged with driving rhythms, the searing electric guitar sound made famous by Muddy Waters and the raspy, edgy vocals of artists like Howlin' Wolf. Guitar rhythms that favoured a heavy backbeat – focusing on the second and fourth beats of every measure – and piano rhythms that drove eight beats to the bar were characteristic of the early R&B sound. The singing was also important, of course. Howlin' Wolf's energy-driven vocals marked one end of the scale while harmonising – based on the style of 1930s, gospel-influenced singing groups like the Mills Brothers and the highly influential Ink Spots – played a strong part in the R&B recordings of the 1950s and 1960s. These themes had their roots planted in early blues music but rock'n'roll took those ideas and ran with them.

Arguments about who released the first rock'n'roll record rage on today, but many fingers point towards Chess Records and Jackie Brenston's 1951 classic 'Rocket 88', which he made as part of Ike Turner and The Kings Of Rhythm. This record, produced by Sam Phillips, was licensed to Chess – Sam didn't start the Memphis-based Sun Records until a year later – and that opened the floodgates for the sound.

Soon afterwards, artists like Chuck Berry were taking the electric guitar sound popularised by Muddy and Howlin' Wolf and upping the tempo. His 1955 Chess release, 'Maybelline', typified this style and became an early rock'n'roll classic. The term rock'n'roll was actually black slang for sexual intercourse, but it's unclear who actually coined the phrase. What was clear was that the emerging teen market loved the music. By the mid-to-late 1950s, white middle-class kids were dancing their socks off to rock'n'roll, much to the distaste of their parents.

By the end of the 1950s, rock'n'roll had swept across America and Europe. Compared with the bland pop music around at the time – US artists like Doris Day and Brit poppers like Cliff Richard were the only alternative – this urban black music was raw and uninhibited. The visceral music and deft production was combined with lyrics that talked about the way people were feeling without just concentrating on puppy love and young people around the world were lapping up these records as fast as they were released. It was during these creatively fertile times, in the mid-to-late Fifties, when the output for American R&B music was equalled only by the appetite for the records being made. That was when rock'n'roll really began to take hold, creating with it the first generation of 'teenagers' and the blueprint of the 'youth culture' of which they were a part. The sound that had its roots in

Afro-American music and that had incubated in cities and towns across America was soon co-opted by European artists. Bands like The Stones and The Who were developing their own take on rock'n'roll and winning their own fans.

The R&B hits of the 1950s were largely released on independent labels and the major labels soon worked out how to cash in on this by releasing covers of the R&B tunes. Such covers, released by the majors, had a more widespread impact than the original. By the end of the 1950s R&B, or rock'n'roll, had been absorbed into the mainstream and came under the banner of pop music.

The aftermath of the R&B era in Chicago was exemplified by what became labelled soul music, a sound which combined secular and gospel musical traditions and added a dose of sophistication and warmth. This style underpinned many of the records cut by Chicago-based artists like Etta James, Curtis Mayfield and Terry Callier and laid the foundation for the Seventies soul scene in America.

Etta James was born in California but lived in Chicago through the Sixties and recorded for Chess Records during that time. Her single 'The Wallflower', released on Modern Records in 1955, had topped the national R&B charts. Her debut for Chess Records, 'All I Could Do Was Cry', was released in 1960 and went to Number Two in the R&B charts and Number 33 on the US national pop chart.

It was through her Chess output that Etta was responsible for some of the early soul hits that came out in Chicago in the 1960s – songs like the upbeat 'Tell Mama', the gospel-fuelled 'Something's Got A Hold On Me' and the luscious 'Trust In Me'. Meanwhile Mayfield, with his band The Impressions, made some of the most exciting and innovative music to come out of the city during this period.

Mayfield started out as a singer and guitarist backing Jerry Butler, but it didn't take long for Mayfield's songwriting skills, ethereal voice and deft guitar-playing to shine through. He had released a lot of his early output through local labels Vee Jay and Okeh, a Chicago soul label that also released records by local soul singers Major Lance and Billy Butler (Jerry's little brother). Jerry and Curtis formed their group

The Impressions in the 1950s and, with Butler on lead, it was their tense ballad 'For Your Precious Love', penned by Mayfield and released on Vee-Jay in May 1958, that marked their first hit. The pair's gospel background and experiences singing in vocal harmony groups formed their early style and this, combined with Butler's pop sensibilities and Mayfield's knack for writing pop-soul, socially conscious songs, meant that they were soon courted by other local labels.

In the fall of 1958, Jerry Butler decided to go solo. Ironically, however, it was his duet with Mayfield, the Vee Jay release 'He Will Break Your Heart', penned by Curtis, that became a hit. Meanwhile, with The Impressions, Curtis hit Number 20 in the pop charts and Number Two in the R&B charts in February 1963 with 'Gypsy Woman', which was recorded in New York and released through ABC Records.

By the mid-Sixties, Mayfield's musical output had become more politically aware. He became Okeh Records' head producer and wrote songs for Okeh stars Major Lance and Gene Chandler. He started his own Windy C label, but this released just seven sides before folding. Most importantly, he continued to pen songs from The Impressions like 'We're A Winner', the civil rights anthem that was banned from the radio in certain parts of the US. In 1970 Mayfield left The Impressions, two years later he released 'Superfly', the soundtrack album to the Blaxploitation movie of the same name. It was widely regarded as his musical masterpiece.

A contemporary of Mayfield's – they lived in the same part of the city and even played basketball together as teenagers – was Terry Callier. Growing up on the North Side of Chicago in the 1950s and 1960s, in the same neighbourhood as Jerry Butler, Major Lance and Mayfield, Terry was open to the influence of much of the same music that had influenced those players. Musically, his early dabblings were immersed in the local R&B scene and Terry was singing in vocal groups from an early age. As a teenager, he would wander the length of Record Row singing his songs for any of the label folk who would listen. Eventually, his efforts paid off and Chess Records signed him up. His style was raw, but it was original and it was a sound that drew from the musical influences that had been nurtured in the city.

It was while wandering along Record Row that afternoon, thinking about the times that Terry must have strolled along that stretch, that I'd determined to look him up. Premonition Records boss Mike Friedman had given me Terry's number so I could get in touch with him.

'You just call him and if he wants to talk to you, he'll call you back. If he doesn't, he won't,' Mike had said.

Terry, known for being a very solitary, shy character, did eventually call me back. It was early evening one night and I was in my apartment sorting out laundry when the phone rang. When I picked up the receiver and Terry answered I knew it was him, even before he told me. I'd heard Terry perform live several times before and, on each occasion, his voice had got straight to my heart. It was the same when I'd listened to his music.

'When I was growing up everybody wanted to be original,' Terry had said.

'Everyone wanted to have their own thing so we were always trying to write new stuff. I started performing vocals when I was about 11 or 12 years old. Just in vocal groups doing amateur shows at places like the Triathlon ballroom on the South Side of the city.'

Terry's first recordings were four tracks for Chess but only one was ever released. 'Look At Me Now', put out by the label in 1963, became a minor hit of the time. Terry is 57 years old now. He was only a teenager when that record came out, and it meant he was making music in the company of greats like Muddy Waters and Howlin' Wolf. He would bump into these stars at the Chess Studios where he also rubbed shoulders with Etta James, on whom he recalls having 'a serious crush'.

'When I was a young man I was socially challenged, let's say,' chuckled Terry. 'It was much easier for me to write down what I felt in a song. Doing it that way meant that I wouldn't have to actually say how I felt to the person, the song would do it for me. It just meant I could get my feelings out there but remain anonymous.'

Terry was just 16 years old when he got a chance to go on tour with the Chess Revue – a collection of artists from the label – but his mother wouldn't let him go. He finished high school and started university in 1962 and that's where he got turned onto folk music. Terry only spent at year at university, eventually ditching his studying and moving back to Chicago where he landed a full-time gig at a local coffee house playing folk music and singing the songs he'd written. During this time Terry would play around the city, testing out his own songs and adaptations of classics of the time. Soon he found other musicians to jam with and eventually formed a band. In 1965 he signed with Prestige Records and recorded his debut album *The New Folk Sound Of Terry Callier*, produced by Samuel Charters. He was only 20 at the time and the folk boom was peaking. But the album didn't get released until 1968, by which time the heat had cooled on the folk scene.

The album didn't have the impact Prestige thought it might but, on home turf, Terry was still gigging regularly in Chicago clubs. In 1970 he joined Jerry Butler's Chicago Songwriters Workshop – the famed co-operative that nurtured the careers of people like Calvin Carter, Chuck Jackson and Marvin Yancy. The following year Terry, alongside CSW member Larry Wade, penned The Dells' US Top 20 hit 'The Love We Had Stays On My Mind'. From that success he continued his music career and signed with Chess Records offshoot Cadet Concept, which was established in the late Sixties. They'd already created an offshoot, Checker, which in 1952 released early R&B sides. The style of Cadet Concept, though, was quite specific, with the music released dedicated to the soul sound that was popular in the city at the time. Callier released albums *Occasional Rain*, *What Color Is Love?* and *I Just Can't Help Myself* through Cadet in the next five years. The albums, produced by Chicago band Earth, Wind & Fire creator Charles Stepney, formed Terry's signature sound of that era. Fusing folk, soul and R&B, it was Terry's lyrics delivered with his warm, honeycomb voice that marked some of his best work.

Terry parted company with Cadet Concept in 1976. By this time, soul music was running head to head with the funk-fuelled disco sound that was popular across America. Next Terry signed to Elektra and released *Fire On Ice* and *Turn You To Love* in 1977 and 1978 respectively. He was still very much in tune with the folk and soul themes that were being usurped in the mainstream by the disco boom and he undertook his first tour of Europe in 1978 before being dropped by Elektra. Soon after he retired from music.

'It was after I listened to John Coltrane that everything changed,' remembered Terry. 'I'd never heard anyone throw themselves into music like that. It was a little frightening actually. I'd heard jazz musicians but I'd never heard a group that committed to each other, and that kind of music. It was overwhelming. I listened to his music solidly, for about a week, then I stopped playing in public and got a job as a laboratory technician. I felt that if I didn't have some of that kind of intensity and ability and commitment then I should do something else for a while. I just played at home. When I went back to the clubs, I was thinking more in terms of the jazz influence. It was about that time that I started doing songs again. Shortly after that I got a chance to record.'

In 1992 UK label Talkin' Loud, an offshoot of major label Mercury, picked up Terry Callier under the direction of jazz fanatic and label head Gilles Peterson. At the time Terry was working as a lab technician and raising his daughter. He came out of retirement to release *Timepiece*, a beautiful, classic album that opened up a whole new generation of listeners to Terry's sound. He has since gone onto release on labels including Verve, Premonition and Mr Bongo. He remains a classic example of a Chicago musician who has redefined himself over the years but nevertheless maintained the main thread of his style. Terry has absorbed folk, blues, R&B, soul and jazz in his 40 years of making music, but the themes of his lyrics have remained the same. These days, Terry says, he writes songs about 'these days'. His driving force is his involvement with his music on a spiritual level.

'It's very hard to find peace and comfort these days so you have to make that with what you do,' Terry said. 'Since 9/11 everything's been tense but it was tense before that – people, government, all of it. It stems directly from injustice done to people.

'When you have poverty and injustice, then anything can happen. People can put up with poverty. They can put up with injustice. People have throughout history. But when you've got poverty and injustice and oppression then you have a very volatile situation. That's what's happening all over America.'

In his hometown, Terry remains an underground phenomenon, loved, cherished and respected by those who know him for his music. He had a regular gig in the city a while back at the Green Mill Pub, the oldest jazz venue in Chicago that was famously owned by Chicago-based gangster Al Capone in the 1920s. The Green Mill was at the hub of the city's North Side jazz scene at the time when the Stroll, on the South Side of the city, was in its heyday. The Green Mill still hosts some of the best jazz players in the city. The low-lit interior – made up of a long, curved wooden bar, intimate wooden booths and a small stage at the back of the room – remains true to the layout of the club when Capone hung out there in the 1920s. Terry did the gig at the Green Mill for a year, playing every week with his Chicago band. You can still hear him play in the city sometimes but these days you're more likely to catch him gigging in London or across Europe.

As I was sorting through my records and CDs that sunny Saturday afternoon, trying to create order out of my messy pile, I came across the CD copy of Terry's *Live At The Mother Blues 1964* that Premonition Records released in 2000. Mike Friedman had given me the album that first time we met, when I'd turned up at his offices in Bucktown. I looked at the cover of the CD, turned it over in my hand, and read the blurb on the back. 'Terry began his sets by lowering his head, closing his eyes and strumming instrumental introductions that went on for minutes', read the snippet of Jeffrey Chouinard's sleeve notes.

I looked at the half-finished job in front of me. I'd decided to sort the music alphabetically by artist, after all, and I wasn't quite at the 'T' section yet. I moved the rest of the vinyl and CDs into a messy pile by the side of the shelf. It had taken me nearly eight hours of sorting, listening, and lounging to get to where I had and I decided I could sort out the rest of my collection another day. I picked up the Terry Callier

CD and my CD Walkman, grabbed the last bottle of beer from the fridge and walked out to the porch at the back of my apartment.

'As I walk down this track, I've got tears in my eyes, tryin' to read a letter from home,' sang Terry in 'Work Song', the first on the album. The melancholy mood of the song, combined with just Terry's voice, accompanied by his guitar and two acoustic basses, hit a nerve. I was miles away from home, just like the song said. But listening to Chicago's soul poet, sucking on a cold beer, watching the raw beauty of the city sunset as it lit the backyards in front of me red gold; home was soon the last thing on my mind.

8 Rock Meets Country

ON THE northeast corner of Clark and Erie, in the northwest of the city, is a long line of posh eateries where you can get anything from home-made pasta to gourmet kebabs. The Bloomer Chocolate Company is based in this area and, any time of day you stroll around this part of town, you can pick up the sweet chocolate fumes pumping out of the building. Known to locals as 'River North', this part of town incorporates the city's largest gallery district and Friday night is a great time to go and check these out, making the most of the weekend-heralding champagne receptions that go on here. Strolling through that part of town in the daytime one day – before the evening cocktail crowd had taken residence – it was clear that this area had undergone gentrification in recent years. Smart boutiques and galleries punctuated the succession of restaurants that filled the area and sitting at the tables that spilled out onto the street were smartly dressed city types, eating, chatting and hanging out in the sunshine.

Wandering the streets of this trendy neighbourhood it's not hard to see, beneath the slick coat of the newer buildings, the bare bones of an area that was once an abandoned warehouse district. The old buildings have been dressed up since this area got regenerated in the early Nineties, but a glimpse of how it used to be can be had in the majestic old Court House Building, on 54 W Hubbard Street, where some of the city's infamous criminals were tried.

Standing on this corner, I realised I was just a handful of blocks from the cosy La Scarola restaurant. This family-run Italian eatery –

where you can choose from plates piled high with delicious pasta as well as other delights – was one of the first restaurants I sampled when I came to Chicago for the first time. If you were to walk from this corner to La Scarola, it'd probably take ten minutes. A taxi would have you there in a spot. But that wasn't the reason I'd strolled to that particular corner in the near North Side of the city after getting off the El at Grand. The real reason I was there lies long buried beneath the trappings of the fancy new restaurant in front of me. As I stood outside this eaterie that particular afternoon, I imagined it as it was a quarter of a century ago. Back then, the building I was looking at was a grungy small Chicago tavern called O'Banions. I'd read about it while scouring the Internet for information on Chicago's music scene in the late 1970s.

The second blues explosion had been and gone. Soul, disco and pop-R&B had taken over the music charts. While blues and jazz were still popular across the city, with local musicians playing in bars and clubs all over Chicago, it wasn't until the late 1970s that the city would see its next important musical revolution. Evidence of this is what I was looking for on the Internet before I arrived in Chicago. Somehow, after hours spent pottering and clicking on links that took me to further links and even more tenuous links, I'd chanced upon a picture of this grotty-looking spot.

The picture – it showed both outside and in – had been taken in the winter. Snow-covered streets and cruel grey skies framed this grungy-looking bar set on the corner where I was standing now. Unlike today, the building back then – the picture was dated 1978 – was surrounded by a graffiti-splattered wall that backed onto a rundown liquor store on one side and a boarded-up shop on the other. Trudging through the snow and picture-frozen in time was a young-looking man in his early twenties, captured just about to go into the bar. His clothes dated him perfectly: large black, hobnailed boots with tight, battered black jeans tucked into the top of them. A leather biker's jacket was dotted with band pins and zipped tightly over a huge, fisherman-style red and black jumper, and a black wool hat was pulled tightly down over his ears with tufts of longish, brown hair poking out of the edges.

The picture of the inside of the bar seemed to me a fairly standard shot, typical of any Chicago tavern of its ilk. A long, narrow room edged with a bar running along one side opened out into a back room that was larger and contained a dancefloor and a small wooden stage. The picture had been taken at closing time. The tavern was empty save for a solitary figure behind the bar, a skinny woman sporting thick black eyeliner, a scruffy black vest and long, tangled, lank brown hair.

The thing that made this bar different from others around the city, all those years ago, was that this was one of the spots where the very first strains of Chicago's punk-rock movement emerged.

Chicago has a rock scene that's as resonant as any other city in America. Bands play every night of the week in a variety of bars, clubs and concert venues around the city. Because Chicago sits right in the middle of the US, geographically, it's always a stop on any band's tour circuit. Add the fact that there are so many places to play in Chicago and you see that whether they're touring, or just playing in the city, a band can find somewhere to gig any night of the week.

Metro is Chicago's main venue where big-name rock acts come and play when they're in town. Metro is set in Wrigleyville, the same area where the city's ballpark is based and with its 1,100 capacity is the spot where local experimental rock band Tortoise – who came up in the city in the early 1990s and are now world-famous – play when they do a gig. Elsewhere the different strains of Chicago rock can be heard all over the city. It's a healthy scene that has its roots planted firmly in the pre-punk, post soul/disco haze of the late 1970s.

American punk-rock of the late Seventies is more associated with New York or LA but Chicago's thriving scene took hold towards the end of the decade and had just as much weight musically as either of those celebrated scenes. Like the punk scenes in London and New York, the scene in Chicago linked the locally fabricated, DIY-crafted music with art and a social and political message. Like punk music that was coming out of the UK and New York, the focus for the bands coming out of Chicago – that would later be labelled 'punk' bands – was aggression. Punk in America and the UK rose as a direct response to a political climate that left young, working-class people disaffected.

Both the UK and the US were in recession by the time 1980 kicked in. Unemployment was high. Many young, working-class people leaving school were faced with the prospect of unemployment or low-paid jobs and their attitudes to this bleak scenario were encapsulated in this new strain of rock music.

In Chicago it was bands like the Effigies, AoF, Bohemia, Da, Strike Under and Naked Raygun that formed in the late Seventies and started playing gigs in taverns around the city that embodied this new, rebellious style of rock. Inspired by the so-called 'new wave' music that was coming from outside the city and fuelled by the social and political struggles they were facing in Chicago itself, these bands made music that was unique to life in Chicago. No one outside of the city knew about it.

The music itself was centred around hard guitar playing, crashing chords with short and basic melodies. The lyrics were disaffected, harsh and hawkish and were often delivered in a violent and bellicose manner. If disco was about escapism, and forgetting everything on the dancefloor, then new wave and punk music was about reality. It was music to fit with the times.

Apart from O'Banions there were other clubs and taverns in the city that nurtured Chicago's first strain of new wave or punk bands. Oz was a floating club that existed at a selection of venues around the city. It started out as a gay bar by day and a punk bar by night but eventually, due to harassment from local police, it was forced to move. After its relocation, it became the hangout spot for young people who were into hearing the resident DJ play sides by bands like The Subverts, The Dead Kennedys, Black Flag and the Upstarts. Local band The Effigies played their first ever gig at Oz in early 1981. Later that year, the band released a five-track EP called *Haunted Town* with the title track – a fast-paced, futuristic lament about a rundown town – based directly on the band's experience of living in Chicago. Their sound came under the 'hardcore punk' banner but their music wasn't so easily classifiable. Their music mutated between fast songs and slow songs. Some of their songs even had a disco rhythm behind them.

In the early Eighties, Oz moved venue again, this time ending up on Broadway. The third incarnation of the bar wasn't as popular as the previous two. The dance room wasn't great and it didn't take long for the crowds to dwindle. The bar was eventually closed down for good by the police, on a night when The Subhumans were due to play a gig.

Before Oz became popular, the early Chicago punk scene was based around a tavern called La Mere Vipere, which was eventually dramatically burned down. Local lore has it that the police – who weren't happy with the music being played down there and the scene they saw emerging from that spot – burned the tavern down themselves. The demise of La Mere Vipere left the crowd – largely made up of new wave fans, wannabe musicians, art students and trendies – looking for somewhere to go. With Oz closed down too, this paved the way for O'Banions to become the new prime hangout for this scene.

The kind of music played by the DJs at O'Banions was similar to what had been played at Oz and La Mere Vipere. New wave and punk songs from the UK and other cities in the US were woven with reggae and ska tunes from that period. Punk and new wave bands from out of town and abroad would come and play at the grotty tavern and by the time the Seventies were at an end, this small, grotty venue was a regular haunt on the gig circuit for this kind of music.

O'Banions and the other small bars and clubs that devoted nights to these bands and this sound started to crop up across Chicago by the time the Eighties were ready to sprout – but still there was no radio airplay for this kind of music.

Throughout the 1970s, radio stations in Chicago devoted airtime entirely to pop and disco songs, soul and R&B music and uniformed US and UK rock. By the late Seventies, disco music, as far as Chicago radio stations were concerned, was all about the Bee Gees, while rock on the radio was all about big-name bands and endless guitar solos. But this budding alternative rock scene in Chicago began to emerge without radio support. It was underground, fresh and exciting, just like the music that was being made.

O'Banions opened in June 1978 and other bars and city taverns like Neo, Misfits and Lucky Number soon followed suit. Then merely a student at the Evanston-based Northwestern University, Big Black guitarist Steve Albini was one of the crowd who frequented these bars. I'd read enough interviews with Albini to know that it was the local bands like Naked Raygun and Da that he heard playing in taverns and clubs around the city that cemented the foundations of his musical tastes. Albini moved from his home state of Montana in 1980 to study in Chicago and never left. He still lives and works in the city today.

Standing outside the former site of O'Banions that afternoon watching well-heeled Chicagoans sipping frothy cappuccinos, I felt the pang of time passing. The area now is the perfect place to have lunch, early evening drinks or dinner but behind the fashionable pavement furniture and slick décor of these emporiums lies an important part of the city's musical history. Duke's comment about how 'they just pave shit in Chicago' was ringing in my ears as I struggled to equate this sunshine afternoon scene with the snowswept, grotty picture of O'Banions circa 1978 that I'd found on the Internet. I resolved to track down Albini, one way or the other, and see if I could get to talk to him about those times gone by.

Finding Steve Albini, it turns out, isn't too hard. Every single day he can be located in the same spot: at his Electrical Audio studios on 2621 West Belmont. The number of the studio is in the phone book and after being told that this would be the best place for me to get hold of him I decided to give him a call. Not realising that the studio number was in the book at the time, I'd actually got the number from a woman called Bettina who owns local independent rock label Thrill Jockey. That label, home to bands like Tortoise, Sea & Cake and local hip hop crew All Natural, started in the early 1990s. Now it's a Chicago institution. It was originally established as a rock label set up to release the music from underground bands in the city – but these days Thrill Jockey goes across-the-board, including rock, alternative, jazz and hip hop acts on its roster.

'If you're signed to Thrill Jockey', a guy called Ben Vida who is in an acoustic, alt-rock band on that label called Town & Country said, you just become 'a Thrill Jockey band'. There is such a thing as Thrill Jockey bands in the city, he'd assured me. After ten years in business, the label's reputation precedes it. Bettina, who's generally a very busy lady, had been kind enough to give me Steve Albini's number when I arrived in the city.

'He's at the studio from midday to midnight every day,' she'd said. 'You should just call him.'

Steve's band Big Black formed in Chicago in the mid-Eighties. They were just one of the local bands from Chicago that made a name for themselves outside of the city. Their *Songs About Fucking* album, released in 1987, was probably their best-known and definitely their best-selling LP. Since the demise of that outfit, Steve has been involved with bands like Rapeman and his current project, going concern Shellac. Like many Chicago musicians, Steve has fingers in many pies. Shellac releases an album maybe once every five years. All the members of the band have jobs outside of the outfit, which means that Shellac make music simply because they want to. Since the late Eighties, Steve has also been working as a producer. He famously produced albums by Nirvana, The Pixies and Jesus Lizard and turned down Courtney Love's request to produce her band's album – although he doesn't like to talk about that.

He bought his current Electric Audio studio in the mid-Nineties, when it was a deserted warehouse. In 1997, the studio opened for business. Before that, Steve had been working on productions at his home-based set-up not far from where Electrical Audio is now established. Since the company moved to the new studio, bands including The Breeders, PJ Harvey and Bush have had their albums produced at the site. In terms of late 20th-century rock music Steve is a living legend. The thought of speaking to him at all left me a bit tongue-tied. When I called his studio, as Bettina had suggested, I was amazed to find that he answered the phone.

'You should either turn up before midday or after midnight if you want to talk,' he'd said, matter-of-factly.

'Before midday then.'

'Fine. Just come to 2621 West Belmont and that's where the studio is. There's a big silver door and just ring that doorbell and I'll be there.'

West Belmont Avenue cuts across the North Side of the city, stretching right from the edge of Lake Michigan in the east across to the outskirts of the city on the west. Walk the length of the street from east to west and you'll cross the Chicago River just below Wrigleyville and go right over the top of Logan Square and into Avondale. This blue-collar neighbourhood is labelled by the 'Not For Tourists (NFT) Guide to Chicago' as 'the new frontier in North Side urban gentrification'. The neighbourhood appears run down, but is dotted with small stores, corner taverns and fast food stops.

The nearest El stop is Belmont, on the blue line. If you walk east on West Belmont Street, go under the bridge as you step out of the subway and continue up the street; you'll find Steve's studio on the right. When I get to the 'big silver door' and ring the bell, I'm amazed that Steve himself answers it. He's shorter than he seems on TV or in photos. He has short, spiky dark hair, wears glasses and is dressed in a scruffy, dark-red boiler suit with an elasticated waist and a thick, metal zip running down the front. He opens the door and lets me in. We sit down in the lobby and, in a very businesslike manner, he gives me the kind of look that implies that he wants me to ask him some questions. I suggest that the best place to start, if anywhere at all, is right at the beginning.

'When I first came here the punk-rock scene was in full swing and it was a very small, insular, but sort of – in a healthy way – very headstrong scene,' remembers Steve. 'I really liked everything about the place. Every time I'd go to see a show I'd see something new. At that time it was still a little bit easier for young people to sneak into bars – now it's virtually impossible. Unless you are 21 you don't get into a bar. When I first got here you could finagle your way in – people weren't looking that closely.'

When the local bands started emerging in the late Seventies and at the beginning of the Eighties, the scene was pretty much centred around those early groups. The bars they played in, the music they played and the records made by bands outside the city and spun by the local DJs formed the basis of a small scene that started attracting a core group of followers. It took a while for Chicago to establish a self-servicing scene around this music.

'Chicago didn't really develop record labels for this music until pretty late in the game,' Steve told me. 'Wax Trax put out a couple of records initially and then they specialised in electronic dance music. They marginalised themselves by creating this industrial dance scene and it was popular within its idiom but it was so stylistically hype-bound, that it was obvious that it was going to burn out. That took the store down. The label took the store down and that was a real shame.'

It wasn't until later on, when independent label Touch & Go moved to the city in 1987, that Chicago established a proper record label base. Before that, remembers Steve, the scene was still very organic.

'The thing that was nice about Chicago's punk scene was that it was very word-of-mouth,' remembers Steve. 'There was a fanzine called *The Coolest Retard*. There was one radio programme: "The Sunday Morning Nightmare". There were these few little touchstones that everybody, sort of, could gravitate towards. This is a huge city. And because it's physically so large and because there was so little binding everything together stylistically, the bands tended to be really weird. The bands were quite different from each other and there wasn't really a single aesthetic.

'In most other places that had really strong scenes at the time – like LA, New York, Washington DC, Boston and Texas, for example, there was a thread of continuity in the sound of the bands. A lot of the bands had either members in common or they had common ancestry or something like that. Chicago had a little bit of that but not as much. The main thing was that none of the bands from Chicago sounded even remotely similar.

'There was a band called Da who were this kind of spooky, gothic, arty band before such terms were thrown around very easily. At that time Naked Raygun were a really unpredictably weird band. Every show was different. For a while there was an electronic noise element in their music that was really confrontational and really nasty sounding. For a while they sort of sounded rockabilly and they had poofy hairdos. Then they had this super-screechy, fuzzy, trebly period. Then there were times when they had this sort of jungle, not jungle dance sound, a bit like jungle as in African "boogada boogada" drums sort of sound. It was really inspirational to see that band.

'What I liked about it was, coming from a place like Montana, I kind of thought that there was this sort of ordained paradigm of music outside in the real world. Montana wasn't the real world. There you are out in the hinterland. So I figured well, when I get to Chicago I'll get to see the way they do it for real. What was inspirational was that every single band I'd go to see was completely different and it didn't instil in me a notion that you had to do things in a certain way. I think if I had been going out to see punk rock bands in LA, or in New York, or in Washington DC, it would have been a completely different experience. All those bands had very, very specific, very rigid stylistic boundaries.

'Now when the hardcore punk scene – and I'm using the extra ironic finger quotes when I say hardcore and punk – started to develop in Chicago, it imported those stylistic and cultural norms from other places. So the "Chicago hardcore punk scene" was slavishly aping the behaviour of, say, the DC scene. That seemed like a complete dead-end to me. And a complete waste of time.'

By this time Steve was already making music with Big Black. He'd soaked up what he believed to be the most cutting-edge and exciting elements of Chicago's early alternative rock scene and was translating what he'd heard and seen into his own sound. While all around him fashion, music and lifestyle were melding to create what became known as Chicago's 'hardcore punk' scene, Steve and the other members of Big Black, were innovating. Steve remembers that time in the mid-Eighties.

'I just ignored what was going on musically in the city,' he says. 'I really didn't have that much to do with it. There were some of those bands that were good and energetic, entertaining, whatever. Big Black, the band I was in, was just one of a number of bands. We weren't particularly popular, we weren't particularly well thought of. I don't think it was a snob thing. I just think that in Chicago there was a lot to choose from. I did kind of think it was unusual that we were getting so much attention, especially overseas. We weren't even the best band in Chicago. Much less the best band in America. Much less the best band in the world. We were one of a number of bands in Chicago that were quite interesting. Chicago, at that time, wasn't even a remarkable city in its density of great bands. There were as many good bands in Madison, Wisconsin, Milwaukee or Minneapolis.'

Shellac, Steve's current band, is signed to Touch & Go Records. It's the same label that released Big Black's *Songs About Fucking* in 1987. Since those early days when the new strains of punk music were coming out of Chicago things have changed. Touch & Go came to the city in the late Eighties and provided local bands with a base for their music. Since then, supported by Touch & Go though not financially linked to them, labels like Thrill Jockey, Drag City and Bloodshot Records have created a strong foundation for the streams of alternative rock music that's come out of Chicago.

Touch & Go's role in the healthy rock scene that Chicago enjoys today is, as far as Steve is concerned, integral. Under the guidance of label owner Corey Rusk, Steve believes without mincing his words, they are 'the best record label in the world'.

'Touch & Go is absolutely pure,' says Steve. 'There's no decision at Touch & Go made on any basis other than what is the right thing to do. There's no band that's ever signed to the label for any reason other than somebody is absolutely passionate about that band and really loves them. Corey does all the signings. It's not so much that they'll hear a demo and think "oh, I really like this music". That has some effect; but the main thing is that the record label exists as a community of people that respect each other. Whereas almost every other record label is concerned on some level with whether or not they are going to make money, Touch & Go is 100 per cent concerned about doing the right thing. 100 per cent. The right thing means that you put out records from people that you hang out with. You put out records from people that you like and that you trust. The record label, as a model for other record labels, is utterly inspirational. They don't use contracts for anything.'

Touch & Go started as an outgrowth of a fanzine of the same name published in Maumee, Ohio, which is very close to Michigan. The Maumee–Detroit access was also one of the early hotbeds of the punk-rock scene in the Mid West. Touch & Go sort of branched out from this style-bound punk rock and hardcore very early on. The Maumee/ Ohio/Detroit scene formed another regional micro-scene for this music. There were gig network connections between Chicago and Detroit. That's how the relationship between the Chicago bands and Touch & Go developed. Then Corey moved here in 1987 and he moved the whole label here. 'That was a real sea change in the Mid West,' says Steve, 'cos when Corey moved from Detroit, suddenly Chicago then had a great record label.'

As well as sourcing new acts from Chicago, the label would often put out music by established outfits. One such band was punk-folk band the Mekons, led by Welsh frontman John Langford. The Mekons had been involved with major labels. They'd been through the mill in terms of wranglings with the 'big boys' in the music industry and it was only when Langford (who'd met a woman from Chicago whome he'd started dating) moved to the city that he came across Corey Rusk. Their meeting resulted in the Mekons releasing music through Touch & Go. The nature of the way in which Rusk's label was run meant that, for the first time in their musical careers, the band were free of hefty contract commitments and able to pursue other avenues in music. Langford began to hang out in taverns around the city and, picking up on some of the strains of American country music he heard played by musicians in these bars, he started to make this kind of music himself. This was the early Nineties and the 'hardcore punk' scene in Chicago had splintered. Strains of that hardcore sound could be found in the city's industrial scene – focused around local bands like Ministry – and the ensuing alternative rock music being made and played in the city. Chicago rock had, according to music journalists and writers from outside of the city, given way to a 'post-rock' movement. To musicians and artists from the city, this term was nonsense.

While *Billboard* magazine were busy calling Chicago 'the next Seattle' – the city that had spawned Nirvana – in Chicago itself the vibrant community of musicians were just making music and playing it in the city. Bands like alternative, indie rock outfit Eleventh Dream Day were coming out of the city. They were originally signed to LA label Amoeba before getting picked up by Atlantic and today, they're signed to Thrill Jockey.

Doug McCombs from Eleventh Dream is also a member of Tortoise. 'Post Rock' was the term applied to bands like Tortoise and Sea & Cake. Tortoise were originally called Mosquito and then went under the name Shrimp Boat. Back then, they included band members Sam Prekop – who later left and went on to form Sea & Cake – and a singer called Liz Phair. It was Phair's solo career that would see her become one of Chicago's best-known alternative rock exports of the Nineties. Her output, along with that of bands like The Smashing Pumpkins and Veruca Salt, broke into the commercial rock scene and hit headlines outside of Chicago. While outside the city, pundits were busy analysing and pontificating on the music from Chicago, within the city limits a new surge of creativity was building steam.

Without realising it, Langford's penchant for old country tunes put him at the peak of what was about to become a wave of interest in this kind of music. Elsewhere in the city at this time, people were beginning to look at country music being played in taverns and bars and beginning to incorporate certain old country songs into more contemporary soundtracks. One of those people was a local DJ called Nan Warshaw. Now Nan co-owns Bloodshot Records, the label that formed in 1993 and became an outlet for some of the most inspiring alternative music to come out of the city in that decade. John Langford formed a band called the Waco Brothers to enable him to exorcise some of his country-themed demons. The Wacos signed to Bloodshot Records in the early 1990s and remain one of the label's flagship acts. Other Bloodshot artists include Devil In A Woodpile and Alejandro Escovedo. The label was also the springboard from which Ryan Adams launched his career.

The ethos behind Bloodshot is to release alternative country music but anyone who checks the roster can see that there's a lot of different sounds that come under that banner. In an effort to make Bloodshot's aim clearer, Nan and Rob, her partner at Bloodshot, coined the term 'insurgent country' to sum up what they put out through the label. Since Bloodshot started in the early Nineties, this style of future-retro music has gained popularity across the US. A magazine called *No Depression*, dealing directly with 'alternative country' music, was established in 1995 to service this scene. Bloodshot Records is just another of Chicago's successful, independent labels to benefit from the strong framework that Touch & Go put in place all those years ago.

After my meeting with Steve that afternoon, I was determined to get to the bottom of what this new surge of 'insurgent country' was all about. And it wasn't difficult. I tracked down the number for Bloodshot Records and, the next morning, took a cab to their office in the north of the city to speak to Nan herself.

IT WAS early when I arrived – around 10.30am – but Nan was already in the office. Dressed in shorts and sturdy boots with a Cramps t-shirt with cut-off sleeves, she was busy tending to her toddler son when I arrived. Her hair was long, tied in a ponytail. Her ears were multi-pierced, with hoops, studs and dangly charms hanging from each lobe. Later she told me she was 41 – but she certainly didn't look it. On her left arm was a large, colourful tattoo of a punky-looking cow playing the drums, with black holes where its eyes should have been.

'My friends and I are old punks that were disillusioned with the state of the commercial music industry,' explains Nan, sipping on a large mug of coffee. 'Punk rock had been co-opted by the major labels and grunge was a big thing. We were looking for something fresh, exciting, something that spoke to us the way that punk rock did when we were younger. We started seeing these bands that we loved that were playing the rock clubs – the divey rock clubs around town. But we noticed that there were a number of bands that all had a thread of old school country running through their music but yet they were still the same bands that were informed by punk and underground rock. Handsome Family, an earlier incarnation of the Waco Brothers, Moonshine Willie, The Bottle Rockets were here a lot – they're from closer to St Louis, but they played here a lot. Freakwater too.

'There was a turning point, I think, in the music scene in Chicago in the early 1980s where up until that point people didn't go out to see local bands. They went out to see the bigger name bands. Then there was this kind of shift where people decided that we had a great scene and started embracing the local bands. And that's kind of when the punk scene in town really started going somewhere and having a sense of community. Really being supported.

'I was already DJing a country night at a little punk rock bar in town. The bar is now called Delilah's – at the time it was called Crash Palace. It was a bar I was hanging out at and I was friends with the owner. I approached him about guest DJing a country night and he knew that some of his regulars would like it, even though he hated country music. When I first approached him it was all like old traditional country – people like Hank Williams, Buck Owens, Patsy Cline – that I was into.

'At the time I was into Clint Black, George Straight and people like that, who I wouldn't listen to today but I was listening to somewhat then. But most of what I was playing when I was DJing was old traditional country. I was throwing in the alternative country that I knew about but there wasn't a lot to choose from. I mean, I was playing some Steve Earle and Jason And The Scorchers and that sort of stuff then too.

'I think that the themes of the music weren't very different from punk rock. They were real life themes. They weren't just self-absorbing themes. So much of the rock was either just love songs or just "all about myself" sort of attitude, whereas the records from the country band I liked told real working-class stories. And a lot of the stories were class struggles without pushing the politics in your face. Johnny Cash and Merle Haggard certainly have a lot of those social themes running through their music. There's lot of that in blue grass music in general and at the time I was probably playing a lot of Carter Family, stuff like that. So it was all about finding that cool, old country and it was exciting because it was fresh and new to us. And it had those themes in it. It wasn't too cool or hip and that kind of made it more exciting because the appeal of it was still underground.

'There were a lot of people who came just to hear that music and those people totally got into it. Some of the regulars who would be in the bar on other nights who would come would be like, "what the hell is this? What are you doing?' But then as time went on, we found some really cool stuff to play that would even draw them in. The Bad Livers, they did a cover of an Iggy Pop song and other bands that did covers of old punk rock songs. The more fucked-up stuff we played, the better it worked. We would throw in some things that were like minded – like some Cramps, stuff like that. Some old rockabilly too; like to kind of help open people's minds to the more country stuff.

'One of the regulars who hung out in that bar was Al Jorgenssen from Ministry. He came that first night I DJed and was just going "this is great, you gotta do this every week" and I said "you tell that to Rick the owner but he doesn't even like country music". He's like "I'll tell him and I'll DJ with you". And so, for the first two years I was DJing there, Al and I alternated Wednesdays.

'We've seen the whole alternative country/roots music or whatever you want to call it scene really grow and flourish here and I don't think we could have done Bloodshot Records in any other city. It's a combination of the fans being here and having great clubs too. And having these club owners that are in it for the music, that treat the bands well and have a really great sense of who to bring in and what bands to put in their clubs and do it right. There's also some great independent record stores in town: Laurie's Records, Reckless Records, Hardboiled, Record Emporium – some are bigger than others. We've seen a lot close over the years too but there are still some strong independent record stores in town.

'We came up with the term "insurgent country". Because at the time we wanted a description that made people think about what we were doing and realise the motion behind it and that it was a rebellious sort of thing. And to make people not just think of the word country and think of the horrible commercial country radio that they hear. When I've had to describe it, I've described it as having a thread of old school country running through it but being informed by punk and underground rock. Most of our artists did play in punk or rock bands before they started playing country. Many of them discovered country music later then brought it into their music. But most of our bands have traditional rock instrumentation. Some of them have steel as well.

Or mandolin. Or some other acoustic or more country-based instruments. But DIAW is more blues-based than any of our other bands.'

The Waco Brothers lie at the sonic centre of what Bloodshot Records do, says Nan. The label's first release was called *For A Life Of Sin – Insurgent Chicago Country*, a compilation of Chicago's underground country bands that the label put out in 1994. Also that year, the label put out a string of 7" releases by the Wacos and Moonshine Willie and then, in 1995, they put out full-length albums by those artists.

The best way to get a dose of what Bloodshot is all about is to go to one of their label club nights. It just so happened that Bloodshot were doing a party that weekend at a venue called Fitzgerald's in Berwyn, one of the suburbs that border Chicago. The Wacos were due to play that night.

When I turned up at the gig, I got a dose of what was so exciting about the output on Bloodshot. Devil In A Woodpile were doing their unplugged, acoustic country blues thing to an audience of thigh-slappers in one of the rooms of the sprawling venue. In the main room, just before he was about to get on stage, I managed to corner John Langford from the Waco Brothers.

'The Waco Brothers started out with me and a friend of mine, Justin Barrs, just playing country songs for a laugh in taverns around the city,' says John. 'It was just the two of us playing covers. Not the novelty stuff – more the serious, Johnny Cash stuff. Also songs by artists like George Jones and Ernest Tubb; stuff like that.

'Country music was just one of my infatuations. Going to Nashville. Going down to Memphis. Trying to wash myself in the history because you go looking for things that really aren't there any more but also you can just be in a town like Chicago which I don't think has anything to do with country music and meet amazing people. I met a band called The Sundowners who were from Chicago and they used to let me get up and play with them. These were seasoned guys who never made it big, but they played. They backed up Tammy Wynette. They were guys who knew all the ropes and they played five nights a week from 11 at night till 4am. We would go down there and they would always get me up to play. At first I was really scared to do it. After I'd done it a couple of times and sung country songs straight, in front of a redneck crowd, who were all drunk, and got away with it, I was emboldened.

'So I did the Wacos. It was really just like a novelty little weird thing to start off with and then Bloodshot formed around the same time and every gig we'd do we'd get a little bit better and we'd have more people. Steve from the Mekons was living here at the same time. He'd been here for quite a while and he left the Mekons and I said, do you want to come and play in this country band we've got? He got his mate Tom Ray in, who was in the Bottle Rockets – he was a bass player. It just kind of turned into this real band. It was just meant to be a band just to play in bars in Chicago but we ended up touring Australia the year before last. It's totally mad.'

Since those early days playing in taverns around Chicago, John admits he's amazed at the interest that's generated around this music. As often happens with outside interpretations of new music scenes, it's the music itself that gets trivialised for the sake of the style and fashions that emerge around it.

'We were trying to do a serious take on country music as opposed to that "cow punk" thing that went on in England, where everyone was blacking their teeth out, wearing dungarees and going "yee hah",' says John. 'To me it's not a laugh. We have a laugh but we're kind of laughing with it. I think there's a lot of funny stuff in country music but I think it's deliberate. I don't think it's a bunch of stupid red necks making some crap.'

The Waco Brothers have released six albums so far with Bloodshot. As they take the stage at Fitzgerald's – a club that's been going for 20 years and that John describes as 'the best club in the world, ever' – the appeal of what they do becomes obvious to me. The music they make is clearly influenced by blues, country music and rock music. John sings while he plays the guitar. Waco classics like 'Poison' and 'New Deal Blues' have the crowd whooping and dancing in front of the stage. The 300 or so people dancing in the dimly lit room as the Wacos play are lit up by strings of fairy lights that hang from the ceilings. On either side of the dancefloor are two moose heads, staring down solemnly over the mayhem. One corner of the room is taken up by a small, squat bar, serving jars of beer while a battered acoustic guitar suspended by wire swings above the pumps. As the Wacos play on, driving the frenzy in the room, a man grabs me by the arm and swings me round. 'You got a lot of Lake County in here tonight,' he grins, whirling me around again.

As John belts out lyrics like 'history is written by the winners' to the whooping crowd, I get the tingling feeling that a heady slice of Chicago's day-to-day history is happening right here on the dancefloor, for this 300-strong crowd, spinning round and round to the music.

9 Outsiders

'WHEN you look at Charlie Parker's biography you see one picture, it's a close-up of Charlie Parker, and there's a Chinese/American piano player in the background. His name is Harry Lim. But to this date there's no documentation about him,' says Tatsu Aoki.

Tatsu, a well-respected bass player in Chicago, tells me this as we sit together at a downtown club called the HotHouse. Tatsu has lived in the city for a quarter of a century; making music with most of the important jazz players in Chicago. Aside of playing the bass, he's been making traditional Japanese folk music for years, and incorporating this music into the jazz sound he loves. He also makes films, most of them short, abstract pieces set to music. His energy is limitless and, because of this, his artistic nature extends beyond his own projects and into the task of nurturing other musicians. One of his concerns is giving support to young and upcoming Asian-American musicians and exploring the place of Asian-American musicians in history. According to Tatsu, Harry Lim played regularly with Charlie Parker and other lauded jazz musicians of that era, yet he's never mentioned anywhere in history books on the subject.

'We as Asian-American musicians – people like myself, Francis Wong and Jon Jang whose first few pieces really claim the rights for the Asian/American to be in the scene – are not really rewarded enough for our contribution to jazz music. Starting from Charlie Parker all the way through to Max Roach and Jon Jang, our contribution to the music has existed. I think I'm the only musician of my time who's made albums with Joseph Jarman, Malachi Favours and Don Moye independently. It's strong evidence that we can claim we have made a contribution to music.'

The HotHouse is located on 31 East Balbo in the South Loop, and Tatsu is scheduled to play his bass in a friend's band tonight. Formerly in Wicker Park, the HotHouse has been at this spot since 1996 and it couldn't be an easier place to find in the city. Back when it was based at Wicker Park, the HotHouse was the cornerstone of the city's experimental jazz scene. The surge in this style of improvised playing and performing happened in the early to mid-1990s and it was the HotHouse that put on a lot of the ensembles and acts that made up that scene. It still hosts bands like that, as well as open mic sessions and the regular Monday night swing jazz slot in which Tatsu is performing.

The nearest El stop to the HotHouse is Harrison on the red line. When you come out of the subway at Harrison you find yourself on State Street. Head south on State, with the El tracks to your left, and Balbo is second on the left. It's in a lively neighbourhood with an 'eclectic bar culture', if you go for standard guidebook definitions. It's true though, there are a lot of places to get a drink around this spot. A watering hole called Kasey's is nearby on 618 Dearborn Street where you can get cold beer and spirits, but only if you're paying cash. Buddy Guy's Legends is just nearby on 754 South Wabash. Every Tuesday there's a farmers' market on Polk & Dearborn and you can get good, cheap meals at Trattoria Caterina on 616 South Dearborn, and at lots of other eateries too.

I had emerged from Harrison just as the sun was setting, dipping behind the buildings that framed the drab steel of the elevated El tracks and lighting the trains in metallic flashes as they zipped past. Most El trains are heavily graffitied and covered in the tags of local street gangs and colourful, spray-painted art. On walls, advertising boards and deserted buildings in the city, Chicago's hip hop culture finds its voice where it can and on the trains you get bite-size bursts of these spray-painted images and slogans as they fly past They are like technicolor movie stills running at double speed. Against the shadowed cityscape, in the final throes of the sunset, there's nothing more beautiful than watching these multi-coloured, metallic snakes manoeuvring the city-dirty elevated tracks, with a whoosh that cuts through the surrounding streets like the strongest Chicago winter wind. Standing there, watching those elevated trains, I got the sense of Chicago as a real American city. Listening to their metallic, heavy lament I realised it wasn't so hard to find echoes of that in the music here. Music is always full of unconscious echoes, but in Chicago these echoes seemed so distinctive to me. The way people talk here. The kind of mechanical sounds they hear.

Just as the sun's parting, gilted-orange flickers were disappearing behind the buildings that evening I was due to meet Tatsu, a train took the bend right where I was standing, just by the Harrison El stop. There in the ochroid glimmer of the approaching evening, I saw something rarely spotted in a cityscene like this: a totally clean train. As each pure, silver carriage whizzed past me, the final flecks of daylight winked out behind the buildings. Perfect timing, it seemed, to go and make the most of the twinkling, glittery night-lights of a city club.

The HotHouse opens at 8pm. I bump into Tatsu just as I arrive, under the brown/red awning of the club that leads to the large, clear-glass front door. He is carrying his double bass with him in a large black case that dwarfs his height by at least two feet. We go in and position ourselves in one of the plush red booths on the mezzanine floor that surrounds the dancefloor and the stage. He seems pleased to see me. He is armed with a large plastic bag full of CDs, pamphlets and flyers that he hands over to me with a big grin. Apart from the club manager and another bartender, setting the bar up and cleaning glasses, Tatsu and I are the only two people in the building.

Tatsu has recorded with local artists like Fred Anderson, Joseph Jarman and The Art Ensemble Of Chicago's Malachi Favours. He has a string of his own albums out too and plays regularly around Chicago and outside of the city and abroad. He's 46 now but his interest in jazz stems from way back, when he was a child growing up in Japan. He's followed and studied the history of the music since then. He moved to Chicago in 1978 to study film at the city's celebrated Art Institute, where many of the avant-garde filmmakers of the 1980s taught in the past. He'd already started playing the bass by the time he applied for a place at the Art Institute and was equally eager to come to Chicago for its strong history of jazz, blues and gospel music.

'I knew all about people like Fred Anderson, Don Moye, Joseph Jarman, Malachi Favours, The Art Ensemble Of Chicago and the AACM,' says Tatsu. 'I knew about Sun Ra. I knew about the blues music. I wanted to be in a city where the city itself had its own sound and tradition. If you live in places like Tokyo, it really has vogue all the time but it doesn't really have the stylistic identity. Chicago has its own style. It seeps into all the music that's made here. Even people like Fred have heavy blues influence in their music. You can hear this when he plays. I wanted to come to Chicago to see these people even though I wasn't really thinking about being a musician at the time.'

When he arrived in Chicago he found a fertile music scene but struggled to find a way to break into it.

'One of the important factors that I found out, in the very beginning, is that when you start to try to play music with all these great people the first thing you realise is that you're not white, obviously. And you're not black. So where does that musical identity really come from? I can be playing the same lick and same phrases as black people play but it doesn't really mean anything. Technically I can do that maybe, but culturally it doesn't mean much. When they do it they have their heritage, they have their legacy so it really kicks in as their own music. White, avant-garde, jazz music has that kind of European influence and they have their own classical tradition in the marriage of the jazz music, which we just don't belong to. So where are we in this map, where we figure out the fact that some of us are Chinese, some of us are Japanese, some of us are Korean, some of us are Indian? When we bring this musical element into the music that we were influenced with, we have our own identity.

'I really didn't think about marrying my cultural influences with music but I just thought: who could I be in this music? To identify our lives and try to express that in the sound? We bring in our own cultural heritage, our cultural legacy, cultural tradition into the music. So here we are.'

Tatsu grew up in Tokyo in a geisha family and, by the age of three, was playing the taiko drum as part of his family's performance repertoire. The history of the drum stretches back around 4,000 years to its origins in China; in Japan, the first taiko drums are recorded around 3,000 years ago.

The word 'taiko' literally means 'fat drum', although the taiko drums themselves come in various shapes and sizes. One of its first uses was on the battlefield, as a means of frightening enemies. The size of the drum meant that it was the only instrument that could be heard across the entire battlefield. These days, however, it's used for non-combative pursuits. Since the 1950s there's been a resurgence in taiko drumming.

In a geisha family, the taiko plays an important part in performance but it's just one of a brace of instruments that geisha entertainers use to do their job. The tradition is currently dying out although, says Tatsu, you can find pockets of it in Tokyo and Kyoto. Geisha families, explains Tatsu, are entertainment families. For Tatsu himself, this involved the whole family devoting their work to music and entertainment. Tatsu remembers how, as a child, he and his family would play instruments, sing and perform for wealthy families in intimate settings. The performers and family to whom they were performing would sing together, dance together and the whole thing, remembers Tatsu, was fairly interactive.

'It was entertainment for wealthy people,' remembers Tatsu.

'All the ladies in the geisha house they learn traditional arts: dancing, singing, instruments. I grew up in those families. So I had to learn these songs. My mother performed them. My mother was 18 when I was born. By the time she was 21, and I was three, we were performing together. I was that age when I started to learn these songs for the performance.'

Tatsu still performs those traditional folk pieces he played as part of the geisha routine in his taiko group in Chicago. The ensemble is called the Miyumi Project and features four drummers playing on taiko drums of different sizes.

'There are slow and fast arrangements but I think the main difference between Western-style drumming and African or Indian drumming is that Japanese drumming is not polyrhythmic,' says Tatsu. 'So, in other words, it's just very simple. We don't really have that kind of complexity in the idea. It's just very simple, steady rhythms. On the other hand, when you have ten of these taiko drummers doing different things, it could sound like an ensemble.'

You can hear the Miyumi Project play regularly around the city. Originally, they performed only within the Japanese community but, since 1996, Tatsu and other Asian-American musicians in the city have been organising an annual Asian-American music festival in Chicago. The festival happens at the end of October every year, right here at the HotHouse. During the summer, Chicago hosts a festival of some sort nearly every weekend. This is just another one of them but, says Tatsu, for himself and other Asian-American musicians in the city, their festival plays an important role in getting exposure outside of their communities.

It's not just traditional Asian-American music that's on the line-up at the festival. Neither is it all jazz-themed. Mia Park is a Korean-American 'rock star' from Chicago who's regularly included on the festival billing. So too is local rap/spoken word group I Speak In Two Tongues, made up of Asian-American rappers and musicians. Chicago violinist Jonathan Chen translates his traditional, Chinese-American-influenced violin playing into the experimental, electronic music he makes and he too is a regular at the festival. It's these younger, rising stars that are important in pushing Asian-American music forward.

'The important part is that education has to take place on this musical movement,' says Tatsu. 'Sometimes Asian-Americans themselves don't realise it. Young Asian-Americans don't realise they're part of the exclusion unless somebody like us points out the fact – to say "look, did you ever think about why we're not in this listing. Why is that? Is it because we're not good enough?"'

However, Tatsu's bass playing is the reason he's at the HotHouse tonight. The simplicity of the taiko rhythms, says Tatsu, translates well into playing the bass, although it's not an instrument he chose initially. When he was at high school back in Tokyo, Tatsu wanted to be a rock star and so he took up the guitar to emulate his heroes from bands like

Deep Purple, Led Zeppelin, Traffic and Pink Floyd. In later teenage years, he became involved in a band with other kids from his school. He was the youngest. They needed someone to play the double bass and he drew the short straw. Now, playing bass is what he's famous for. Still, while playing the bass with musicians like Fred Anderson – he features on Anderson's *On The Run* album out on Delmark – Tatsu says that strains of his cultural background – his Asian-American-ness if you like – can be identified.

'I do bring this Eastern, Japanese element to the music,' says Tatsu. 'On the Fred Anderson album, I am more repetitious on my bassline than a Western musician would be. A lot of times when I play I think I perform a more minimal kind of bass playing, where I don't really play loud lines but I keep the same motif for a long period of time. It's very different from some other bass players that have a lot of different lines to play. My lines are a lot simpler, but the time-consuming long ideas and subtle changes gradually change the overall sound over a long period of time. It's those aesthetics that I've brought in for a lot of projects. Even if I'm playing in somebody else's band I think I bring in that kind of idea.'

Chicago, like many other big cities in America, is a collision of cultures and creeds – but with strong neighbourhood distinctions within the city, it's often difficult to get musicians integrated. Tatsu started out playing music within the local Asian-American communities. He and his friends, when they were new, young musicians in Chicago, tried to get gigs or sit in on sessions at local taverns and clubs around the city, but it wasn't happening. Tatsu says they were handed the usual excuses like 'you're not good enough, come back when you are' or 'I'll give you a gig when you've practised more'. In a city where chances to play live have traditionally come thick and fast to new young musicians, Tatsu says that he was amazed to find that neither he nor his friends got the gigs they'd been promised. And so in true Chicago style, even though they were just newcomers to this working ethic of the city, Tatsu and his friends adopted a do-it-yourself policy.

'We just found places to play within our community,' remembers Tatsu. 'That's what you have to do. Then we started recording our own music. If no-one else wants to help out, what choice do you have? You make your own albums, using basic recording equipment. You find the cheapest way to make your albums, then you send these albums out. You create and produce your own shows. You get these places, you advertise yourself. You produce yourself.

'I think one of the interesting things about us in Asian-American music is that we all were able to self-produce and self-promote. If you think about all these Chinese immigrants in America, they were able to come here and they were able to create their own economic bases with Chinatown. It's very much – I wouldn't just say Asian – but it's a very stereotypical immigrant action to take. You really don't have anybody to help you out, so you go around to your community and try to encourage your community to do something with you. By the time I finished my second album, someone from Germany contacted me; a label called Sound Aspects. They're no longer in business. They wanted to do an album with me so I thought: "cool, I'll do it". I did the *Sound Aspects* album. Then a request for a third one came from Asian Improv Records in San Francisco. I continued relationship with Asian Improv Records after that. Southport Records picked up on my music next. Now I have projects here and there with a number of record companies. I'm even on Delmark Records now.'

It's through his relationship with Asian Improv Records that Tatsu hooked up with Francis Wong in San Francisco, where the first ever Asian-American music festival happened in the mid-Eighties. Now, through connections across America, Tatsu has been helping promote the Asian-American presence in Chicago music. The Chicago Asian-American music festival started in the city in 1996. Yoko Noge's Jazz Me Blues Band, who are warming up on the stage just as Tatsu says it's about time he did the same, are a regular feature at the festival. Yoko, Tatsu tells me, has one of the best jazz bands in the city. The band has been going about seven years and its regular Monday night session, here at the HotHouse, is one of the busiest nights in the city. As the band warms up, all the booths surrounding the dancefloor are full. The three-deep layers of smaller tables and chairs that frame the mezzanine surround are filling up too.

Yoko Noge's Jazz Me Blues Band is a swing jazz outfit. Yoko sings in Japanese and plays the piano alongside a horn section and Tatsu on bass. Yoko's band translates swing standards into Japanese as well as adapting traditional Japanese folk songs into this style of playing – and always gets everyone swinging.

On stage I can see Yoko preparing herself. She's tiny and very pretty with short, dark, straight-bobbed hair and sparkly, dark eyes. For the performance Yoko is wearing a cute black dress and a red flowing scarf. The rest of the band is dressed in matching black trousers and yellow-and-red-print Hawaiian shirts. I recognise the trombone player as John Watson, an older man who used to play in Count Basie's band back in the Sixties. From this distance, behind his dark shades and long, grey, beard, Watson looks at least seventy. In fact, confirms Tatsu, all the members of the horn section are in their seventies.

As Tatsu leaves me to warm up with the band, I sip on a cold beer and read the sleeve of Yoko's CD *Yoko Meets John*. Released in 1999 on Yoko's own Jazz Me Blues label, on the cover is a picture of her and John Watson, sitting in a busy Chicago café. Yoko, it turns out, was born in Osaka, Japan, and came to Chicago in 1984. She'd already had success as a recording artist back home with a pop song called 'Ossan Nanisurunya' which means: 'what are you doing, you dirty old man'. The song is about crowded train commuting in Japan and Yoko wrote it in high school. Japanese trains are notorious for being packed and the guys on them are 'always doing crazy things'. Yoko says she was a victim of that. She was shy at the time and couldn't say anything, so she made a song out of it.

'Ossan Nanisurunya' came out on Victor in Japan in 1975. It was around that time that Yoko started developing an interest in the blues. She'd been given an Elmore James record by a friend at college and was already interested in American folk music but when she heard the James record, she says, 'something clicked'. She sourced records by artists like Big Mamma Thornton, Koko Taylor, Muddy Waters, Howlin' Wolf, Bessie Smith and Ma Rainey and eventually discovered a small blues scene in Osaka centred around 'tiny joints' run by collectors of blues music.

She formed her own blues band doing covers of the classics that she loves, often singing the lyrics in Japanese. Then, in 1984, she came to Chicago. Her first gigs were in West Side and South Side clubs where she sat in and sang with blues greats like Willie Kent and Johnny B Moore. She started out singing in English, just doing covers. In 1993 she took up the piano, then she formed her own band and started developing her sound.

As Yoko and the Jazz Me Blues Band play that night, the impact of the Japanese folk songs teamed up with swing jazz music is amazing. It's just gone 8.30pm but the HotHouse is packed and a handful of couples are dancing the traditional, varied-stepped, swing dance. The crowd is mixed in every way. Blacks, whites, Asians and Hispanics of all ages are swishing partners to the music. People in couples are swapping partners for each dance. Some people who arrive alone are selecting other solos for their ensuing dance. Next Yoko sings in Japanese to a familiar tune. The main lights are low. Delicate spots swirl around the band, the dancefloor and the booths. John Watson jiggles as he plays his trombone. The grey-haired clarinet player blows his horn with his dark shades and black beret firmly in place. At the back Tatsu plucks his bass, holding time for the band as the growing, multi-ethnic crowd swishes in front of the stage and across the floor.

DESPITE all of the excitement when the band took their interval my eyes wandered out of the window down onto the street below and I felt a pang for my small apartment, back in Wicker Park. It was just after 9pm. I finished my drink, glanced quickly over to the band, caught Tatsu's eye with a nod – I never was much good at goodbyes – and left.

Down on the street clusters of friends were bustling out of the subway, cars and cabs and into the now-busy bars and restaurants. I took a cab just as a couple got out, clinging to each other in the warm night breeze. The ride back up to Wicker Park was quick and easy. Just as the taxi got to the intersection where Duke's bench was, I decided to get out. Duke wasn't there of course, having long gone back home to wherever it was he went back home to. I looked around at the taxi queue and a couple sitting on the edge of the fountain kissing. I glanced over at the man sitting by his cart selling honeycomb, nuts and sweets. No-one seemed to notice me so slowly, and nervously, I made my way over to Duke's bench and sat right in his spot.

I looked up at the large, round, milky moon and back down at its reflection in the cool dark pool of the fountain. Around me the traffic whirled, cars revved engines, horns sounded, vehicles stopped and started – but here, in Duke's spot, all was calm. My mind wandered to the enigmatic man to whom I'd become so peculiarly attached. I was sure Duke must be nearly eighty himself, just like the men in the horn section I'd seen play in Yoko's band tonight. In fact, just like so many of the other old jazz and blues players I'd come across in the city since I'd arrived.

When Duke was in his twenties, the whole stretch of Division Street, around this intersection, was dotted with taverns. Most of them were just drinking dens with juke boxes, he'd said. But there were a couple too where piano players and singers performed or smaller combos played the bebop-style jazz sound he loved, to bawdy customers. Back then the area around his bench was surrounded by run-down, wooden tenements where families would live four, sometimes five, to a two-bed space. As a kid Duke sold newspapers on the corner of Division and Ashland, just near where his bench is now. He was tiny, he remembers, and his small pile of papers were stacked on the floor, held down on top by a stone. In the winter he remembered freezing on that corner, the wind biting through his thin coat, but he would stay out, long after dark, until all the papers were sold. He didn't remember specific tunes he heard in the taverns around that time. Duke just remembered enjoying the music, after a hard day working, which was nearly every day.

In a way, Duke was typical of the Chicago experience. Chicago had been a conundrum when I arrived. For a city that has played such an important role in the history of music, Chicago didn't seem to make much of its heritage. Thousands of tourists turned up each year to make their pilgrimage to the city but Chicago itself seemed unperturbed by the attention. Apart from the chi-chi trappings of

Navy Pier, with its big wheel, restaurants and bars, there were no airs and graces to Chicago. People were neither rude nor saccharine friendly in this city. Instead, when they chose to show it, I had felt a genuine warmth, something comfortingly real. That afternoon, Duke and I had chatted and I'd asked him why he thought Chicago didn't celebrate its history more. All these people who had lived and worked here, who had passed through here, and who right here in the city had made and recorded some of the best music of our time? I thought about his reply while I was sitting there in his spot, on his bench, that night after Yoko's gig at the HotHouse.

'Well I'm not a big plaques and memorials guy myself,' Duke had said. 'Better enjoy things while they're happening and celebrate people while they're around, don't ya think?'

It was Monday. I remembered that Tortoise guitarist Jeff Parker's jazz quartet was playing at The Green Mill that night. The man selling the honeycomb, nuts and sweets was packing up his cart for the evening. I looked at my watch. It was nearly 10pm. I walked over to the first taxi in the queue opposite Duke's bench, opened the door, got in the back and told the driver where I was going.

Appendix 1

Sounds, Tastes and Things To Do

TWENTY OF CHICAGO'S HOTTEST MUSIC VENUES

ABBEY PUB
Local alternative rock acts most nights of the week with alt country
bands regularly guesting here too.
3420 West Grace Street
Tel: 773-478-4408

B.L.U.E.S. and B.L.U.E.S. ETCETRA
This is one of the most prominent North Side blues clubs where all the
big names in blues come to play when they're in town. The second
venue, Etcetra, is larger and less intimate than its sister venue.
2519 North Halsted
Tel: 773-528-1012 and 773-525-8989

BLUE CHICAGO
The two branches of this blues club are just a short walk from each
other and one cover charge – around $5 – allows entry into both
venues, where good blues music from city players and out-of-town
guests is hosted every night.
536 North Clark Street
Tel: 312-661-0100
736 North Clark Street
Tel: 312-642-6261

BUDDY GUY'S LEGENDS

Buddy Guy's venue in the near South Side is good if a bit grotty and the big names in blues play alongside lesser knowns. Cover charge varies depending on the night and you can get food here too.
754 South Wabash
Tel: 312-427-0333

CHECKERBOARD LOUNGE

This South Side blues club is one of the best in the city with live blues every Friday and Saturday night. Get a cab from right outside the club to head back uptown when you're finished.
423 East 43rd Street
Tel: 773-624-3240

EMPTY BOTTLE

Local alt-rock acts and improv jazz players can be heard nearly every night of the week here. Cover charge varies depending on who's on but this is a trendy, bustling place to go for a beer, whatever you're into.
1035 North Western
Tel: 773-276-3600

FITZGERALDS

It might be a bit of a hike from downtown but well worth it to hear alt country, folk and blues bands.
6615 Roosevelt Road, Berwyn
Tel: 708-788-2118

GREEN MILL

A *must* while you're in Chicago. It was once owned by Al Capone and, for a small cover charge, you can hear live jazz here every night of the week. The décor has stayed true to the venue's original incarnation and, if you ask the manager nicely, he'll pull out a scrapbook complete with newspaper cuttings of the Green Mill's long history.
4802 North Broadway
Tel: 773-878-5552

HIDEOUT INN

Set just west of Lincoln Park, this bijou, two-roomed venue is host to local band Devil In A Woodpile's Tuesday night hoedown, as well as a string of other DJ-led, live music run nights. No cover charge on most nights, so prepare to put some dollars in the hat when it comes round at the end of the night.

1354 West Wabansia Avenue

Tel: 773-227-4433

HOTHOUSE

Jazz and blues are regularly featured here to varied cover charges and this is definitely the place to head if you like slicker surroundings to hear your music in. Check out the cocktail list too.

31 East Balbo

Tel: 312-362-9707

HOUSE OF BLUES

This venue plays host to big acts that make it to the city – both rock and blues – and what you get here is the less intimate, more slick-packaged experience. Check out the gospel brunch on Sunday morning for as-much-as-you-can-eat food and a flashing-lights, gospel choir extravaganza.

329 North Dearborn

Tel: 312-923-2000

JAZZ SHOWCASE

This candlelit jazz bar is one of the best in the city and is run by hardcore bebop fan Joe Segal. Cover prices are high but the acts are good and Charlie Parker month runs every year for the whole of August.

59 West Grand Avenue

Tel: 312-670-BIRD

KINGSTON MINES
This large venue is one of the best that contribute to the North Side blues scene in the city. Open till 4am every morning and a great place to hear lives blues with a drinking crowd.
2548 North Halsted
Tel: 773-477-4646

METRO
This 1,100 capacity, multi-level venue is where all the better-known dance and rock acts play when they come into town.
3730 North Clark Street
Tel: 773-549-0203

THE NEW APARTMENT LOUNGE
This neighbourhood-bar style venue is as laid back and relaxed as the regulars that drink there. There's no cover charge and if you're going to venture way south to get here then do it on a Tuesday night for local tenor sax man Von Freeman's weekly session.
540 East 75th Street
Tel: 773-483-7728

RED DOG
One of the best clubs in town for dance music – hip hop, funk and especially house. Open every night.
1958 West North Avenue
Tel: 773-278-1009

ROSA'S
This West Side blues club provides live music from Tuesdays to Sundays and you can get some down home blues alongside bigger acts here at this Italian-American run venue.
3420 West Armitage
Tel: 312-342-0452

SLICK'S LOUNGE
Open every night, this is the place to go and hear/dance to house music in the city.
1115 North North Branch
Tel: 312-932-0006

VELVET LOUNGE
This South Side jazz venue, run by local tenor sax player Fred Anderson, is an institution in the city and one of the best places for the Chicago jazz experience. Cover charge varies depending on who's playing.
2128 South Indiana
Tel: 312-791-9050

ZENTRA
House music emporium that books the cream of local and international DJs.
932 West Weed
Tel: 312-787-0400

TWENTY RESTAURANTS

AL'S NO. 1 ITALIAN BEEF
Carnivores get your meat here. Good prices too.
1079 West Taylor Street
Tel: 312-733-8896

BOXCAR CAFÉ
This café is right near the Magnificent Mile shopping area and the lake front but, unlike many of the eateries in this area, it's reasonably priced. Smoothies, hot and cold paninis, ice cream and coffee are on offer and, if you're eating, you can use the Internet for free too.
1166 North Lasalle
www.boxcarcafe.net

DEMON DOGS
Chicago hot dogs at their best, just a stone's throw from the baseball ground.
844 West Fullerton Avenue
Tel: 773-281-2001

DON QUIJOTE
If you like burritos as big as your arm, then get down to this uptown joint.
4761 North Clark Street
Tel: 773-769-5930

HAROLD'S CHICKEN SHACK
THE best chicken restaurant in the city, right in the heart of Bronzeville. Tasty prices too.
364 East 47th Street
Tel: 773-285-8362

HILARY'S URBAN EATERY (HUE)
Good, healthy, vegetarian and meat-eating joint.
1500 West Division
Tel: 773-235-4327

JOE'S BEBOP CAFÉ & JAZZ EMPORIUM
Another of Joe Segal's jazz venues but this one is bigger than the Showcase. Set in the chi-chi Navy Pier, it serves food and drink. There's music every night and a Sunday jazz brunch that's worth a go.
Navy Pier, 600 East Grand Avenue
Tel: 312-595-5299

LA SCAROLA
Authentic Italian food at reasonable prices in a warm, friendly atmosphere.
721 West Grand
Tel: 312-243-1740

LAO SZE CHUAN
There are many restaurants to choose from in the East
Pilsen/Chinatown area but this offers authentic food and evening
karaoke. Your chance to do a rendition of Frank Sinatra's 'Chicago'?
2172 South Archer Avenue
Tel: 312-326-5040

LULA'S
Hipsters munch on pan-ethnic nosh at this Logan Square spot.
2537 North Kedzie Boulevard
Tel: 773-489-9554

MAX'S ITALIAN BEEF
This place is a Chi-town institution, not least for the pepper and egg
sandwich.
5754 North Western Avenue
Tel: 773-989-8200

MIRAI SUSHI
Slick dining and good sushi.
2020 West Division Street
Tel: 773-862-8500

NOOKIE'S TREE
Set in the East Lakeview area this diner is open 24 hours. Cheap and
cheerful but good food too.
3334 North Halsted
Tel: 773-248-9888

RHAPSODY
European and American cuisine that hits around the medium price
range. Good wine list too and this restaurant is attached to the
Chicago Symphony Hall.
65 East Adams
Tel: 312-786-9911

SMOKE DADDY
Barbecue ribs and blues music every night.
1840 West Division Street
Tel: 773-772-6656

STAR OF SIAM
This restaurant is good for lunch, dinner, cocktails and carry-out/delivery and is one of the best and most reasonably priced in the city. Right round the corner from the Jazz Record Mart too.
11 East Illinois Street
Tel: 312-670-0100

THE CHEESECAKE FACTORY
Sweet toothers alert! There are over 40 kinds of cheesecake for sale here. Mid-range prices but worth it.
875 North Michigan
Tel: 312-337-1101

THE PUMP ROOM
This is a dress-for-dinner affair with high prices to match – but if you want some old school-style Chicago dining then this is the spot.
1301 North State Parkway
Tel: 312-266-0360

TRU
Expensive but worth it: this place is as much about being seen as it is about eating food.
676 North St Clair
Tel: 312-202-0001

UDUPI PALACE
Vegetarian Indian food with a good low-fat menu option and at a reasonable cost.
2543 West Devon Avenue
Tel: 773-338-2152

TWENTY PLACES FOR THE CHICAGO EXPERIENCE

THE ART INSTITUTE OF CHICAGO
Without argument one of the best art museums in the world. This spot, on 111 South Michigan Street (Tel: 312-443-3600) has an art collection that spans 5,000 years with Grant Wood, Picasso, Monet, Renoir and Gauguin all represented.

BAPTIST CHURCHES
From Salem down South to Pilgrim Baptist Church, the best way to get the full-on gospel experience is to go along to a service. As they say, all are welcome.

BASEBALL AT WRIGLEY FIELD
Home to the Chicago Cubs, built in 1914 and the second oldest ball park in Major League Baseball – you have to visit it on 1060 West Addison Street. You can get tickets for a Cubs game via the Cubs website (www.cubs.com) or by calling Tickets.com on 800-843-2827.

BOYS TOWN
Despite the name, this isn't just for the boys. Based around 3000 N Halsted the string of bars and restaurants make it one of the liveliest areas in the city.

BRONZEVILLE
This pocket on the near South Side of the city was where much of Chicago's jazz music of the early 20th century was played. The once thriving African neighbourhood features monuments to this including the 'Walk Of Fame', a stretch where musicians Louis Armstrong and Nat King Cole are among those commemorated. Check it out in the daytime then get a bite at Harold's Chicken Shack. Blues emporium Checkerboard Lounge and jazz haven Velvet Lounge are in the neighbourhood so you can take your pick.

CHICAGO BOTANIC GARDEN
Stroll around these sublime gardens at 1000 Lake Cook Road to get away from the hubbub of the city.
Tel: 847-835-5440

CHICAGO RIVER TOUR
Take your pick of city river tours that offer a calm float through the towering skyscrapers that make up the downtown area of Chicago and out of the city, further up and downstate. Odyssey Cruises (Tel: 630-990-0800) are just one of the companies that do it – but shop around for the best deals.

DU SABLE MUSEUM OF AFRICAN-AMERICAN HISTORY
Opened in 1961 and named after the city's first settler, this museum tells the story like it is. Blues and jazz fans will be interested as much of the history of both kinds of music lies here.
Tel: 773-947-0600

EVANSTON
This suburb is only 13 miles from the city's busy loop area but with its prairie-style homes and tree-lined streets you could well be hundreds of miles away. Restaurants, museums, shops are all in the downtown area but there's no real buzz to this part. Perfect for a day away from the city.

FAMOUS GRAVES
If graveyard antics are your thing you can visit the graves of Muddy Waters (Restvale Cemetery on 115th and Leamington) and Howlin' Wolf (real name Chester Burnett whose grave is in Oakridge Cemetery on Roosevelt between Manheim and Wolf Road).

FAMOUS HOMES
Louis Armstrong's former home, where he lived on and off from 1925 while he was married to Chicago singer Lil Hardin, is at 421 East 44th Street. Muddy Waters's former house is at 4339 South Lake Park. You can check out Benny Goodman's place at 1125 South Francisco Avenue too.

THE JAZZ RECORD MART
This jazz and blues emporium is a must-see in the downtown area on 444 North Wabash.
Tel: 312-222-1467

LAKE MICHIGAN
Sunbathe and swim anywhere along the Chicago stretch of Lake Michigan or you can take Lake Tours. There are too many to list so shop around for best prices and exactly what you're looking for.

LUNCHTIME JAZZ AT ANDY'S LIVE JAZZ
This jazz club, in the heart of the Loop, has been here for over 20 years and is one of the best places to hang out and hear jazz while you eat and drink. Small round tables face a stage that sits next to a large, centrally placed bar; you get early and late sittings for jazz every day. Pictures of the greats that have played here cover the walls and acts span generations of jazz music.
Tel: 312-642-6805

MAXWELL STREET MARKET
Not what it used to be but still worth a visit if you fancy some tacky stalls and buskers on a Sunday morning. It recently moved from its original site to Canal Street.

NAVY PIER
Based at 600 East Grand Avenue, this pier is a hive of activity with the Family Pavilion, Crystal Garden, Ferris Wheel and Skyline Stage linked by a string of bars and restaurants. Nice for an evening stroll.

OUTDOOR FESTIVALS
Chicago has outdoor music festivals happening in its many parks all over the summer period – from May to October – covering Jazz (Tel: 312-744-3315), Gospel (Tel: 312-744-3315), Blues (Tel: 312-744-3315) and more.

SECOND CITY COMEDY CLUB IN OLD TOWN
This famed improv club was where the likes of Rick Moranis, Mike Myers, John Belushi and Bill Murray got started. Check it out, set in this historical area.
Tel: 312-337-3992

SHOPPING ON MAGNIFICENT MILE
Gucci, Prada, Max Mara – they're all here on this stretch, going from the top end of North Michigan Avenue southwards.

THE VIEW FROM THE TOP OF SEARS TOWER
Combine shopping and views at Sears, on 2 North State Street. Order cocktails or coffee at the top of this vast tower.

Appendix 2

Hotels, Getting There and Getting Around

TEN CHICAGO HOTELS

Accommodation in Chicago isn't cheap and you need to book in advance, especially during the summer season:

CASS HOTEL
Budget hotel with budget rooms but great option if location and a place to rest your head is all you're after.
640 North Wabash
Tel: 312-787-4030

FAIRMOUNT
Singing waiters complement the elegance of this beautiful hotel. Sublime surroundings at a price. The adjoined Primavera restaurant is great too.
200 North Columbus Drive
Tel: 312-565-8000

HOUSE OF BLUES HOTEL
Attached to the House Of Blues venue, this is a music-lover's option with exotic, blues-themed rooms. You pay for it too.
333 North Dearborn Street
Tel: 312-245-0333

HOUSE OF TWO URNS B&B
Cosy, arty, Wicker Park B&B that offers a cheaper and less corporate alternative to the big chain hotels. Yummy breakfasts thrown in too.
1328 North Wicker Park
Tel: 773-235-1408

MOTEL 6
If you like the motel experience then you'll get it here, although the usual motel prices don't apply in this case.
Chicago Downtown, 162 East Ontario Street
Tel: 800-466-8356

RADISSON HOTEL & SUITES CHICAGO
Great downtown location for this mid-range priced chain.
160 East Huron Street
Tel: 800-333-3333

THE SENECA HOTEL & SUITES
Formerly an apartment block and now a hotel with around 50 rooms and as many suites. Mid-range prices for those who like their rooms spacious.
200 East Chestnut Street
Tel: 312-787-8900

W LAKESHORE DRIVE
Chi-chi wing of the 'W' chain where every room is a design classic. You pay for it but it's worth it for the views across Lake Michigan.
644 North Lake Shore Drive
Tel: 773-943-9200

THE WILLOWS
If neighbourhood hotels are your thing, then this mid-range hotel offers cosy rooms and continental breakfast to boot.
555 West Surf Street
Tel: 773-528-8400

WICKER PARK INN B&B
Right in the middle of this vibrant neighbourhood, this 1890s-built, quiet B&B is comfy. Prices are mid-range but worth it.
1329 North Wicker Park
Tel: 773-486-2743

GETTING THERE

BY PLANE

Chicago has two airports:

O'Hare International
In the northwest of the city, O'Hare is the busier of the two Chicago aiports and most international flights land here.
Tel: 773-686-2200

Midway
This is just ten miles southwest of the downtown area.
Tel: 773-838-0600

Cabs from both airports cost a standard rate to downtown Chicago – around $30 – and you should find out how much before setting off on your journey. Otherwise buses and shuttles to and from downtown run regularly.

American Airlines and United Airlines do cheap flights throughout the year, ranging from around £250 in the cheaper post-Christmas/pre-spring season and up to £600 or more during summer and leading up to Christmas. Go to www.americanairlines.com or www.united.com. Most other major airlines fly to and from Chicago's airports and you should shop around for deals.

BY BUS

Greyhound Trailways
If you're travelling to Chicago from somewhere else in the States or Canada you can get Greyhound buses. Greyhound's main station in the city is at 630 West Harrison St in the West Loop. The bus service, called 'the dog' by locals, is very cheap and basic, so wear comfy clothes and take things like pillows and food if you're going on a long journey. There are toilets on board but make sure you pack your own toilet paper.
Tel: 312-408-5980

GETTING AROUND IN CHICAGO

TAXI

Taxis are cheap and run 24 hours in Chicago. You can always find yellow or white taxis to flag down in the street and there are a string of taxi companies that do call-out services.

BUS AND TRAIN

The Chicago Transport Authority (CTA) buses and El Train Transits are all air-conditioned and very cheap, with lines covering the city. Tickets cost around $1.50 for a single journey but you can get a weekly travel pass for $20 which allows you free, unlimited travel on all CTA buses and El train routes. Both buses and El trains run very frequently and until well into the small hours but, if you're travelling around at a late hour, the Night Owl buses are a safer option than the El. The El tracks run underground, street level or elevated above the streets and pavement and the colour-coded seven lines that make up the transit system trace a line around the loop before stretching across the city.
Info: 312-664-7200

Metra Line Trains
These trains – covering a dozen lines and 495 miles of track – stretch out much further than the CTA or El train routes, taking you to the suburbs of the city and even further. There are 230 Metra line stations scattered throughout the city and the suburbs. Trains are slower than the CTA services – running every 30 minutes or so – but fares are cheap and if you're heading out any kind of distance this service is a lot cheaper than getting a taxi.
Info: 312-322-6777

Free Trolleys
This is the slow way to get around but the open-air, colour-coded five-line trolley system is great if you want to take it easy and sightsee while you ride. The trolleys run every twenty minutes during the warmer months of the year. Make sure you look out for the 'Free Trolley' sign in the window because fare-based trolleys do run in the city but once you see that sign, you can hop on and off as you please and don't need a ticket to travel.
Info: 817-244-2246

Bibliography

The Apollo Chorus Of Chicago (Apollo Chorus Of Chicago, US 1997)

Not For Tourists Guide To Chicago (Happy Mazza Media LLC, 2002)

ALGREN, Nelson – *The Neon Wilderness* (Seven Stories Press, US 1986)

BREWSTER, Bill, and BROUGHTON, Frank – *Last Night A DJ Saved My Life* (Headline Book Publishing, UK 1999)

BROTHERS, Thomas (editor) – *Louis Armstrong, In His Own Words* (Oxford University Press, US/UK 1999)

COOK, Richard, and MORTON, Brian – *The Penguin Guide To Jazz* (Penguin Books, US/UK 1992)

DU NOYER, Paul (editor) – *The Illustrated Encyclopedia Of Music* (Flame Tree Publishing, UK 2003)

GREGORY, Hugh – *The Real Rhythm And Blues* (Blandford, 1998)

KNIGHT, Richard – *The Blues Highway New Orleans To Chicago* (Trailblazer Publications, 2001)

TOOZE, Sandra B – *The Mojo Man* (ECW Press, 1997)

TRAVIS, Dempsey J – *An Autobiography Of Black Jazz* (Urban Research Institute Inc, 1983)

UNTERBERGER, Richie – *Music USA The Rough Guide* (The Rough Guides, US/UK 1999)

Index

Maps

The first of the following three maps shows the city of Chicago in its entirety, orientating the traveller to some of its major streets and neighbourhoods. The next two maps focus in more detail on the North Side and South Side respectively, with numbered red dots locating the 20 hottest music venues from Appendix 1.

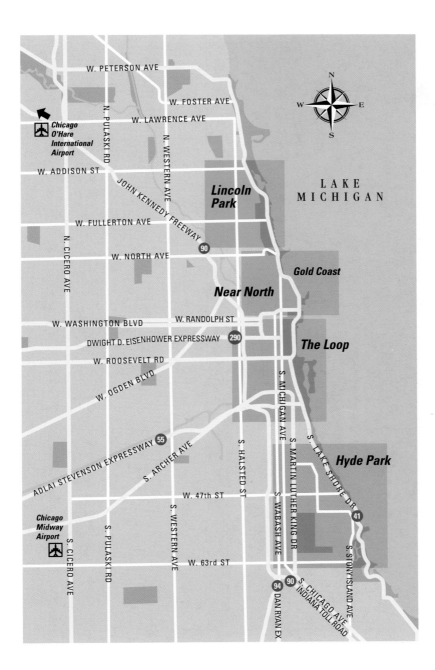

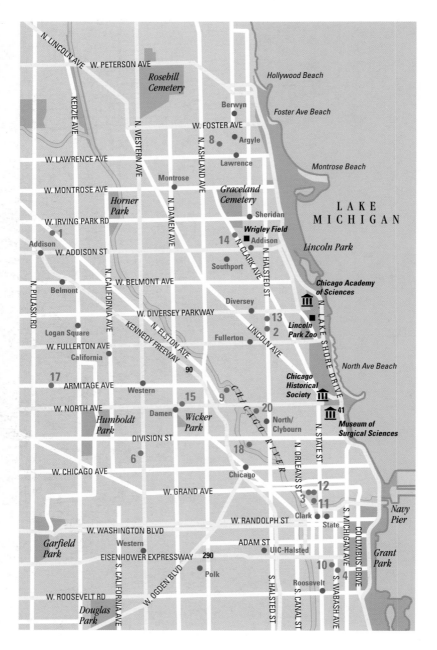

1	Abbey Pub	6	Empty Bottle
2	B.L.U.E.S.	7	Fitzgeralds
3	Blue Chicago	8	Green Mill
4	Buddy Guy's Legends	9	Hideout Inn
5	Checkerboard Lounge	10	The HotHouse